STRUCTURAL APPRAISAL OF TRADITIONAL BUILDINGS

Structural appraisal of traditional buildings

Patrick Robson

Gower Technical

Published by
Gower Technical
Gower Publishing Company Limited
Gower House
Croft Road
Aldershot
Hants GU11 3HR
England

Gower Publishing Company
Old Post Road
Brookfield
Vermont 05036
USA

British Library Cataloguing in Publication Data
Robson, Patrick
    Structural appraisal of traditional buildings.
    1. Great Britain. Buildings. Structural conditions.
    Surveying
    I. Title
    692

Library of Congress Cataloging-in-Publication Data
Robson, Patrick, 1941-
    Structural appraisal of traditional buildings/Patrick Robson.
      p.   cm.
    Includes bibliographical references, and index.
    1. Building inspection. 2. Building failures. I. Title.
TH4 39.R63 1990   90-46066
690'.21--dc20   CIP

ISBN 0-566-09081-3

Printed in Great Britain by
Billing & Sons Ltd, Worcester

Contents

Figures

Tables

Preface

The purpose of this book is to promote the science of structural appraisal, which has its own discipline, different from design. Like design, it needs an understanding of material behaviour, but its essence is detection. There are no formulae for detection, no theories which deduce cause from damage. There are only methods for converging on the right answers. These require visual skills, to which verbal discussion cannot always do justice, and a large number of illustrations have been included to leaven the text.

The book is intended for the general practitioner who has at least an elementary knowledge of structures and foundations, and for the structural engineer who has an interest in, but possibly limited experience of, structural defects and their causes.

The scope of the book is limited to traditional building as it is known in the UK. The same principles can be applied to modern steel and reinforced concrete structures, but an understanding of their detailed behaviour needs specialist knowledge. They also apply, obviously, outside the UK, but the combination of soil conditions, climate and building tradition is unique to every country, and a book which relies on specific examples cannot help being parochial.

The book is based on practical experience, which is never gained alone. My colleagues at the Richard Jackson Partnership have helped me in many ways: sharing their knowledge, improving our ways of prying into distorted buildings and not least by carefully collecting and presenting the primary evidence for numerous investigations. I should not like to have attempted the book at all without the help of my partner, Paul Mellor, who prepared the illustrations from the thin evidence of an early draft.

Two others read the early draft (not the final one, I should say on their behalf) and gave me invaluable advice: Mike Rowell, Director, RSA Geotechnics Ltd; and Mikael Rust, Partner, Rogers and Grundy (chartered surveyors). Vincent May, Managing Director of V. J. Adjusters Ltd, and Bob

Baldock, Director of Training, National House Building Council, both read selected chapters and offered constructive advice. Vic Day (Managing Director, D&H Buildings) broadened my education with much practical advice. I am grateful to them all for the improvements they made.

My wife managed the book's progress and typed the manuscript, more than once, and, believe it or not, persuaded me to eliminate some of the more obscure passages.

Acknowledgements

The chapter on monitoring has been adapted from an article by the author published in *Construction Repair* (now known as *The International Journal of Construction Repair and Maintenance*) Vol. 1, No. 3, August 1987.

Extracts from BS 5628: Part 1: 1978 are reproduced with the permission of BS1, Linford Wood, Milton Keynes, ME14 6LE.

Chapter 1

INTRODUCTION

Whereas design and supervision are mainly analytical tasks, structural appraisal is detective work. Often, it is a bad investigation which demonstrates this distinction by failing to observe it. An investigation which inspects, but does not diagnose, will merely produce a list of building faults, and will recommend, or imply, that each one should be corrected. That is seldom necessary.

Designers must equip new buildings to face uncertainties during their useful life and, for design purposes, these uncertainties are codified. The designer refers to British Standard loading, approved details and regulations, and accepted margins of safety. There is no such guide for investigation. The same codes cannot be applied in reverse because their uncertainties would get in the way. The object of investigation is to determine what has really happened.

Although investigation loses the comfort and security of codes and standards, it gains the advantage that the damaged building is its own prototype: observe its behaviour and you have seen it tested.

Unfortunately, not all its behaviour is visible. In fact, it is difficult to inspect a building thoroughly without vandalizing it, because many of the important parts are hidden behind coverings and decorations.

There is no avoiding the need to establish the cause of damage. Without it, future action is a gamble. Since every effect has more than one potential cause, interpretation is a process of challenge and elimination. This is where many come unstuck, hence the list of faults or, just as bad, the idiosyncratic judgement, biased by a narrow experience of defects.

There are many types of investigation, of differing purpose, some comprehensive and some with only an incidental structural interest, and there are many types of building, but the process of challenge and elimination can be applied to all. The effort varies, of course. The first decision an investigator has to make is what to investigate: how to tailor the work to suit the occasion. There is no need to take a checklist to every plaster crack.

Most traditional buildings have a scale, in their room sizes and storey heights, which shields them from catastrophe or progressive collapse, so that there is time for the investigation to be thorough, the work being under no more than the usual commercial pressures of time and money. The great majority of investigations are of safe buildings.

Some do become unsafe, either through accident or abnormal sensitivity, or, occasionally, some insidious problem such as hidden decay. Their investigation has to be *ad hoc*, and urgent. When safety has been restored, their future, if they have one, is likely to benefit from the same methodical enquiry as safe buildings.

Chapter 2 outlines the principles of investigating safe buildings – the collection and interpretation of evidence – but conclusions cannot be manufactured from observation alone. They must draw from a fund of knowledge of the common causes of structural damage. These are discussed in Chapters 3–6. Their effect on the superstructure is often influenced by the foundations, a point which is discussed in Chapter 7.

Techniques for collecting evidence are discussed in Chapters 8–12. Chapters 13–17 discuss interpretation, including the less straightforward cases where the evidence is inadequate or the damage is sudden. The monitoring of movement and damage progress is considered in Chapter 18. Investigation attracts liability, as does any form of professional advice, and means of managing it are briefly discussed in Chapter 19. Chapter 20 summarizes the main decisions on the path to appraisal.

Chapter 2

PRINCIPLES:
SAFE STRUCTURES

The key to sound appraisal is the correct identification of the cause or causes of structural damage. When this is known the matters which are more important to the client – severity, prognosis and recommended action – easily fall into place.

For the purpose of investigation, cause should have a narrow technical definition. Reviews of building practice may refer to design faults, and reports on individual buildings may blame something more specific such as 'shallow foundations', and both may be correct in their context. But plenty of design faults and shallow foundations survive for their useful life without causing damage, and an investigation cannot stop at either point.

For damage to occur, something must have caused movement. It is that event which the investigation must first uncover. Later, the circumstances which could be criticized for aiding and abetting the event may be of equal interest, but they must not be allowed to confuse the detective work. For example, a gable wall may be described as 'lacking restraint', and that may well be correct, but if the wall has stood for decades before succumbing to damage, it would not be an adequate description of cause; neither would it lead to a useful recommendation. The singular event must be identified first.

The singular event could of course be a combination of movements – for example, thermal expansion and foundation settlement. But as a general rule, structural damage has only one major cause, if we define major cause as the event without which damage would not have occurred. A building may well suffer from several problems, each with its own major cause, but it is not usually difficult to recognize their individual symptoms and isolate each cause.

Rarely do two causes contribute equally and simultaneously to the same damage.

Returning to simple major causes: Figure 2.1 shows a very straightforward case of masonry cracking, but from a visual inspection alone the cause is not obvious. Several interpretations are possible: the right hand end could be going down; the left hand could be going down; both ends could be going down; the middle could be coming up. These four possibilities cover foundation movement. In addition, we may need to consider thermal or moisture movement, and there may be other potential causes related to the superstructure alone.

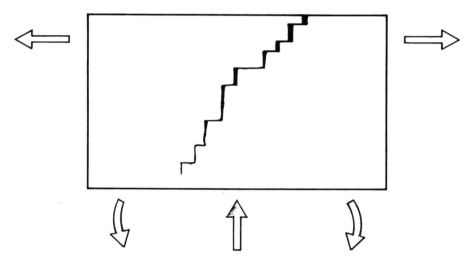

Figure 2.1 *Simple masonry damage*

Interpretation is even harder when the symptoms are less straightforward. Figure 2.2 shows a two storey wall with openings. It is undergoing subsidence. Diagrams (a) and (b) show alternative responses. In diagram (a), cracking is initiated at eaves level and propagates diagonally downwards as the end of the wall rotates anti-clockwise about foundation or ground level. In diagram (b), cracking starts along a bed course close to ground floor window head level, where adhesion between mortar and masonry unit happens to be weak, leading to a more local rotation or possibly shear movement. It would not be difficult to imagine several other plausible crack patterns arising from the same movement. Cracking starts at the position where tensile stress first exceeds the strength of the masonry unit or mortar or bond between the two.

Masonry is heterogeneous. Various small but incomputable variations, such as the weak adhesion imagined for the sake of Figure 2.2(b), can influence the pattern and even the timing of cracking. So maximum stress need not occur where the structural engineer would predict, and cracking need not occur at

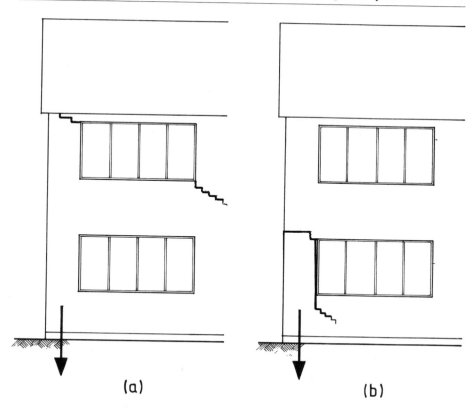

Figure 2.2 *Alternative responses to subsidence*

the position of maximum stress. These uncertainties make it difficult to work back along the link from effect to cause; visual evidence is imprecise.

The same is true of all evidence. The best of it should be regarded as second rate, and even that status should be accorded grudgingly, no matter how much care has gone into its preparation. In Figure 2.2, information can be improved in detail by, for example: recording the width and taper of each crack and any shearing along its line, any tendency to be wider in perpends than bed course or vice versa, and any out of plane movement across the crack; assessing mortar grade including variations; looking for signs of poor adhesion; noting any evidence of ageing of crack surfaces; assessing properties of the masonry unit; noting the quality of restraint provided by floors and cross walls; and so on. Useful though this information often is, it is never conclusive as to cause. The law of diminishing returns puts an early brake on observation: the more sophisticated it becomes the greater its burden of irrelevant information. We need a technique for interpreting unsophisticated evidence. There is a very simple one, fortunately, based on finding compatibility between evidence taken from different viewpoints.

Figure 2.1 shows masonry damage with a number of potential causes. If levels are taken along a mortar bed, using surveying equipment, any departure from the horizontal would imply that foundation movement may be the cause of damage, and if the pattern of departure is well defined it may be possible to judge the direction and degree of movement. Figure 2.3 shows the same case, with relative levels plotted on the elevation. In itself, the level survey is not conclusive because it contains inherent variations which are unknown, but it becomes powerful when used in combination with the visual evidence. The power comes from the compatibility check.

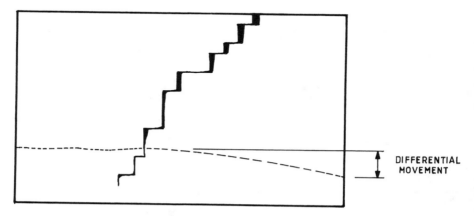

Figure 2.3   *Damage related to movement*

Every potential cause of damage should be judged against every piece of evidence. Those causes which do not survive scrutiny can be eliminated. What remains is the truth. The more viewpoints, or techniques, which are used, the more certain will be the interpretation.

The most useful techniques are as follows:

- desk study
- visual inspection
- distortion survey
- monitoring
- testing
- circumstantial evidence.

Returning to Figure 2.2: a desk study might have established the likely ground conditions; a distortion survey should have located the subsidence and provided a rough estimate of foundation movement; monitoring could have been a means of testing whether it was progressive; testing would have established the properties of the ground below foundation level and any variation from place to place; and lastly, circumstantial evidence might have been powerful enough to rule between apparently similar causes – for example, if the building is old and the cracking new, foundation movement would be due to subsidence rather than settlement under load.

Not every case needs the full treatment. Not every investigator can apply it and not every client can afford it. There are short cuts which can be used if the loss of accuracy is tolerable. For example, using Figure 2.2 again, a spirit level or string line might have been used instead of a precise level, in deciding whether foundation movement had occurred. The information would have carried less weight, of course, because of its reduced accuracy.

Once the cause or causes of damage have been identified, establishing severity and prognosis requires only a little more effort. They tend to be characteristic of the cause, and they benefit from the same work, although additional detailed information may sometimes be required in the way of soil testing or monitoring, or whatever.

Severity of damage can be judged empirically by appearance or more accurately by the degree of distortion and loss of integrity, if these have been recorded. Monitoring can establish whether the damage is progressive, but when the cause is known with confidence it is seldom necessary to monitor for that purpose alone. Monitoring may be a useful check on recovery or settling down, after the cause has been removed.

When cause and severity are known, it is possible to consider future options. In the case of Figure 2.2, supposing the cause to have been subsidence due to leakage from a water main, the choice would lie between repairing the leakage and allowing the subsidence to work its way out, or underpinning the foundations to a stable stratum. Those alternatives represent opposite ends of the severity spectrum. Intermediate remedies could be considered, such as local foundation stiffening, depending on the detailed circumstances. When movement has either ceased or been arrested, the damage to the wall can be repaired and any lost integrity with floors, roofs or other walls can be restored if necessary. As the damage is in this case, particularly in diagram (b), simple and local, it might be practical to eliminate at least a proportion of the distortion by jacking from a firm base, if that is thought to be worthwhile. Once safety has been assured, detailed action is usually influenced by many non-technical considerations.

The options for remedial action, in ascending order of damage severity, can be summarized as follows:

- do nothing (movement extinct)
- remove the cause but otherwise do nothing (favourable response expected)
- remove the cause, await stability and restore integrity (building weakened but favourable response expected)
- remove the cause, carry out improvements, await stability and restore integrity (damage mildly progressive)
- arrest further movement by underpinning or partial rebuilding or replacing failed elements and restore integrity (damage seriously progressive).

To the extent that information is limited, inaccurate or flawed, there is a residue of uncertainty about the conclusions. The compatibility check is the best way to define this uncertainty when it exists. Unless the information can be improved, recommendations should have to take into account the effects of all the potential causes which have not been eliminated, so that the boundaries of safe action can be determined.

Although compatibility is the essence of interpretation, it can only operate from the firm base of a thorough understanding of building defects. This knowledge provides the stock of potential causes of damage which is the equivalent of the designer's references.

Chapter 3

CAUSES OF DAMAGE: SUPERSTRUCTURE

The purpose of this chapter is to outline the common causes of structural damage which arise from above-ground loads and hazards.

Wind loading

The cause of severe wind damage is seldom in doubt, but it is sometimes necessary to establish the reason why a particular component failed. Minor wind damage, on the other hand, is not always seen straightaway, and when it is seen later its origin is not always obvious.

It is impossible to calculate storm conditions after the event, but the nearest weather station will usually have a record of gust speed and wind direction at its own location, and specialists in meteorological effects can estimate local pressure coefficients with fair accuracy. But for most circumstances a general understanding of the main factors is sufficient. Storm damage is influenced by wind speed, local topography and structural details.

The basic UK design speed (gusts exceeded once in 50 years) varies from 38m/sec in southeast England to 54m/sec in northwest Scotland, and may be increased by topography and degree of exposure. Most damage in the UK is caused by wind blowing from within 45° of due west, and most damage occurs from November to February.

Wind accelerates up shallow escarpments, shallow being defined as a slope which is no steeper than 17° in the direction of the wind. Its speed can be up to 60 per cent higher at the crest than at the bottom. The difference in speed between high and low is roughly the same when the wind blows in the other direction, down the hill. Only with steep hills is there any significant shelter leeward of the crest.

Valleys are sheltered from winds which blow across them, but winds blowing through them, especially from the lower and wider end, will accelerate.

Buildings enjoy shelter from vegetation and from local buildings of similar size, but they can be exposed to high pressures, possibly twice as high, from deflections caused by tall buildings downwind. Passages of low ground between high buildings are like valleys, and can create severe wind forces.

Buildings with well-restrained roofs and walls rarely suffer from wind damage in the UK. Their greatest risk is usually from falling trees and flying debris. Occasionally, progressive failure can occur even with well-constructed buildings, and this generally starts with local damage caused by excessive gusting. For example, a low-pitched roof may lose tiles and vital structural connections at its verge, where wind suction is greatest, and this would expose both roof and gable to increased pressures after having severely reduced their edge restraint.

Progressive failure is not very common, however. Damage is usually confined to individual components which have been let down by a specific weakness, and the most vulnerable of these are: unrestrained flat roofs and gables; weak chimneys; projections and canopies; balconies and parapets; and walls with large openings.

Low-pitched, especially flat, roofs are probably the most vulnerable components of all. In severe cases, wind may remove the roof altogether, or at least peel back part of it. Nearly always, this happens because the roof structure is not adequately tied down to the supporting walls.

Brick gable walls are also vulnerable unless strapped to the rafters and joists, and they may peel away from the apex, or fold along a bed course. A gable wall with a cavity may lose only its outer skin if the inner one is restrained. This often happens when the ties between leaves are few in number, poorly embedded or weakened by decay. The greatest threat to gables comes from wind channeled between buildings.

Projections may be levered off a building by severe wind uplift. If their roof joists continue across the enclosed part of the building, the resulting damage can be devastating.

Chimney stacks stand up well if they are in good condition, but if they have deteriorated through attack by frost or by sulphates in the bricks or flue gases they may succumb to severe gusting.

Buildings with large openings on the windward side suffer increased pressure on their roofs and on their leeward walls. In that particular case, uplift is actually higher for pitched roofs than flat roofs, although the former usually have more dead load with which to resist it.

Less serious wind forces may cause local cosmetic damage, whose origin is not always obvious if it is not noticed at the time. In the case of parapets, movement during wind may damage flashing, which may not be noticed until later, when rain penetrates through to the top storey. Projections and canopies can cause unnoticed flexing or even temporary uplift at the external wall support, and cosmetic damage along the ceiling line (Figure 3.1) is not an uncommon sight. Sometimes a flat roof is left, as a result of its disturbance, with a small permanent upward tilt at whichever corner received the brunt of the uplift. Occasionally, walls register horizontal cracking along a weak mortar bed.

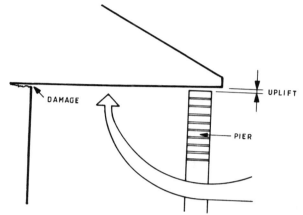

Figure 3.1 *Wind damage*

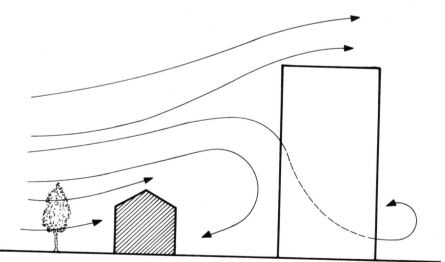

Figure 3.2 *Environment and wind*

Environmental changes can sometimes account for why wind damage occurs to buildings which had previously withstood decades of storms. Referring to Figure 3.2 as an apocryphal example, if shelter is removed upwind of the shaded building and a tall building erected downwind, the risk of wind damage is certain to be magnified.

Snow loading

Snow rarely causes major structural damage except where the roof profile encourages drifting (Figure 3.3). The British Standard (BS6399: Part 3) is a useful commentary on this effect, which was underestimated until the 1988 revision.

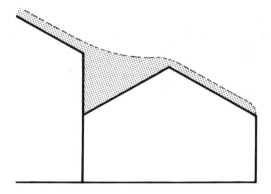

Figure 3.3   *Snow drifting*

Sliding snow is a hazard to gutters and on rare occasions causes structural damage. If the lower roof in Figure 3.3 were long and steep the party wall might be at risk from impact by a layer of sliding snow. Alternatively, snow from the higher roof could tip onto the lower.

A roof which has been insulated and reclad with, say, tiles replacing slate, may have to sustain not only heavier dead weight but slightly longer and heavier loading from snow settling on the colder roof surface. That would rarely be dangerous, but it might increase distortions.

Roof self-weight

Many traditional roofs are undersized by modern standards, even under normal dead loading, and this is betrayed by the visible distortions of principal members. Rafters usually suffer most. It is not unusual to find original fractured rafters still in place but augmented by new pieces of timber. Sometimes weak areas are found strutted off an internal wall or healthy-looking joist – or anywhere.

Rafters may rest on purlins whose spans are too large to offer useful support, although they do, even when grossly distorted, provide useful wind bracing in that plane. They also add to the roof's overall stiffness, typically by 20 per cent or so, by redistributing loads between rafters of unequal value. Such purlins may look tired but should never be removed unless replaced by something better. Binders often 'support' ceiling joists in a similar way, and to similar effect.

Even grossly distorted roofs are usually safe, if they are old enough to have stood the test of time and are not facing environmental changes, but a small further weakening by decay or alteration may introduce doubts. Improvement, not to modern standards but at least to the original level of safety, is usually simple and economic unless the internal appearance of the roof space has to be preserved at all costs.

Other vertical roof loading

Re-covering can be the signal for new problems in an old roof, particularly if the dead load is increased. Members weakened by rot or insect attact may deflect more than previously, or even fail. Softened wall plates and loose joints may exhibit a greater than expected degree of bedding down when the full load is replaced.

A flat roof may over deflect if rainwater forms ponds on its surface. Ponding can result from inadequate falls or deflection under dead load (in which case the additional effect of ponding could well be alarming) or blocked gutters. Blockage is a perpetual menace if all the rainwater is not collected at the perimeter. Flat roofs with easy access are prone to abuse. Material stacking is the most dangerous.

If the structural members of timber flat roofs do not stay dry they will eventually fail. Rot due to interstitial condensation is found most frequently in cold deck roofs where the insulation, if any, is below the roof deck. Rain can penetrate a membrane which has failed through differential thermal movement. That tends to be a warm deck problem, where the insulation lies immediately below the membrane. Blistering or simply inappropriate bonding or sealing can also let the rain in.

In most cases of condensation and penetration, the damp is recognized as a problem to be cured before it leads to structural failure.

Roof spread

Pitched roofs should be tied at eaves level, the purpose of the tie being to resolve horizontal forces at rafter feet which might otherwise cause roof spread. Nearly all modern buildings have this tie. Many older buildings do not.

There are occasions when the lack of tie is unimportant. If the majority of loading is supported by purlins (Figure 3.4), which are themselves adequately supported – remembering that some are so feeble as principal members that they merely serve as bracing – then the vertical and horizontal load at eaves is too small to cause trouble. Certain mediaeval roofs, such as Crown Post and Queen Post, transfer relatively small load to the external walls. Braced collar roofs may help the wall top to resist spread, provided all the timber joints have remained serviceable.

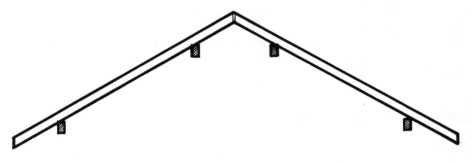

Figure 3.4   *Roof supported by purlins*

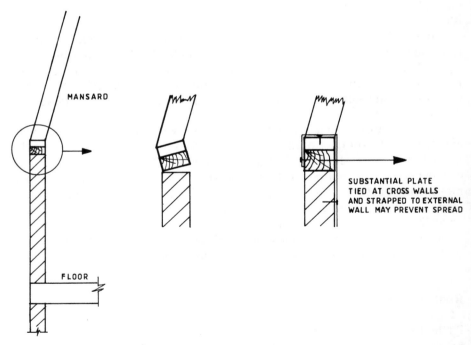

Figure 3.5   *Mansard spread*

Mansard roofs create a much lower horizontal force than single pitched roofs. This is easily resisted if the mansard springs from floor level. If, however, it springs from mid-storey height, and if the supporting wall is masonry, then there may be a tendency for the wall plate to roll or slip unless it is restrained (Figure 3.5).

In typical pitched roofs the tie force is most conveniently transferred from rafter to joist by nailed or pegged connections. In some roofs, this connection is simply not made, even though rafter and joist sit side by side on the wall plate, with the result that the horizontal force can only be transferred by static friction (rafter to plate and plate to joist), which is hardly ideal. In wide roofs, the joists which take the tie force may span across the roof in two or more lengths supported on internal walls. If the joists are not nailed, pegged or strapped together where they meet internally (Figure 3.6) then the tie force cannot be assured. Sometimes separation can be detected at the internal support where the joists abut or lap. This is a measure of spread.

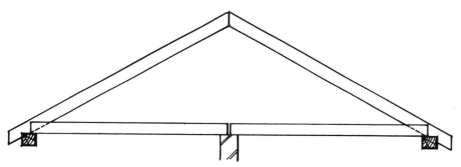

Figure 3.6 *Interrupted tie*

Hipped roofs face the problem that half the jack rafters are not parallel to joists, in which case the tie needs something more positive than a nailed eaves connection. Timber or metal straps, which connect with the rafters and pass beyond the hip region, where they can be nailed to a number of main joists, are satisfactory.

In all cases of inadequate ties, and there is one yet to discuss, the result is roof spread. A horizontal load is taken by the top of the wall, which is comparatively flexible in that plane, and the wall may bow outwards. Old buildings often display this movement gracefully. Much twentieth-century masonry is too brittle to be graceful, and often gets shunted along bed courses.

Roof spread occurs as soon as the tiles or slates are fixed, and thereafter creeps, so it can be regarded as a mildly progressive defect, although it rarely becomes dangerous. If the roof is re-covered, the spread can be regenerated, leading to fresh damage.

The most immediately recognizable example of an untied roof is the sloping ceiling, where joists (which may be called collars) are above eaves level. Spread depends, then, on the bending stiffness of wall and rafter (Figure 3.7). In some cases the weakest rafters cannot take their share and they may fracture in bending.

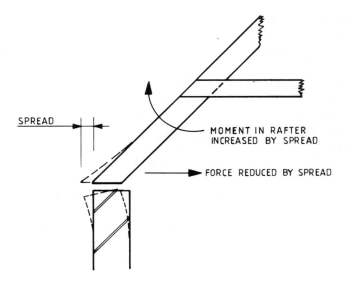

Figure 3.7   *Collar roof*

A roof structure that can tolerate a certain amount of horizontal movement will minimize damage to itself and supporting walls. A typical example is the rolling of a clasped wall plate (Figure 3.8). These wall plates are often large, and their inertia may be enough to absorb virtually all the initial movement and force. Further creep movement may occur, however.

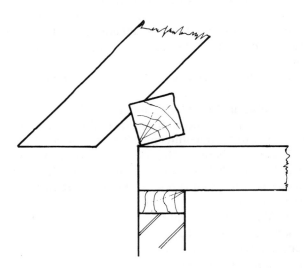

Figure 3.8   *Plate roll*

At positions where the roof span changes direction, as is normal in buildings which are not mere rectangles in plan, roof spread may operate in line with one wall (Figure 3.9) causing vertical masonry cracking. This is sometimes mistaken for foundation movement.

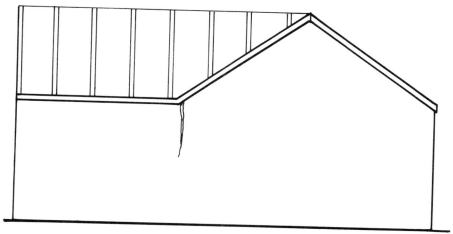

Figure 3.9 *Masonry damaged by roof spread*

Weakened masonry

Most reports make little or no mention of the strength of masonry. This tacitly recognizes the fact that masonry has ample reserves to perform its structural function for many years, regardless of minor movement and wear and tear.

The defects most often named in reports are cracking and bulging. Cracking is an important symptom of damage, although the wall itself usually recovers from it fairly easily, and bulging is a symptom of possible instability which may require more urgent attention. (See Chapters 14 and 17.)

A minority of cases benefit from an assessment of the true compressive strength of the masonry. For example, a proposed alteration may threaten to make greater demands on load bearing walls. In that case, the procedure is similar to design. The wall would have the strength of its individual units, modified by a number of strength reducing factors. If the calculation is critical, it would normally be performed by a structural engineer who would apply safety factors to cover the remaining uncertainties about material properties and loading.

The most obvious, but least observable, strength reducer is slenderness. BS5628: Part 1: Table 7 gives the effect on permissible compressive stress of variations in wall thickness, load eccentricity and distance between supports (or restraints). In order to apply the factors correctly, Section 4 of the standard should be read in full. Table 7 (reproduced in Table 3.1) gives immediate insight into the way strength rapidly diminishes when slenderness rises beyond the typical scale of traditional buildings.

Table 3.1   *Capacity reduction factor*

Slenderness ratio h_{ef}/t_{ef}	Eccentricity at top of wall, e_x			
	Up to 0.05t (see note 1)	0.1t	0.2t	0.3t
0	1.00	0.88	0.66	0.44
6	1.00	0.88	0.66	0.44
8	1.00	0.88	0.66	0.44
10	0.97	0.88	0.66	0.44
12	0.93	0.87	0.66	0.44
14	0.89	0.83	0.66	0.44
16	0.83	0.77	0.64	0.44
18	0.77	0.70	0.57	0.44
20	0.70	0.64	0.51	0.37
22	0.62	0.56	0.43	0.30
24	0.53	0.47	0.34	
26	0.45	0.38		
27	0.40	0.33		

Note 1: It is not necessary to consider the effects of eccentricities up to and including 0.05t.

Note 2: Linear interpolation between eccentricities and slenderness ratios is permitted.

The influence of slenderness highlights the difficulty of inspection. Slenderness may be greater now than it was at the time of construction, for example as a result of loss of bond caused by a previous movement which is now extinct. This would not be apparent if present decorations have disguised the movement.

Unexpected examples are sometimes found of walls which have always been outside the traditional scale. End of terrace gables are often not tied at any of the floor or roof levels. Facades may never have had proper connections to internal cross walls or even to floors, if the joists span parallel to them.

As with old roofs, it is often possible to carry out low cost improvements, not necessarily up to modern standards, but at least to original standards, by tying walls back to floors, or strapping them to cross walls, or introducing other means of hidden anchorage. For these slenderness reducing improvements to be effective, the restraining elements have to be capable of transmitting the small stabilizing forces through the building and down into the ground, and of course the connection details need to be adequate. Figure 3.10 gives a visual summary of the more common strength reducers.

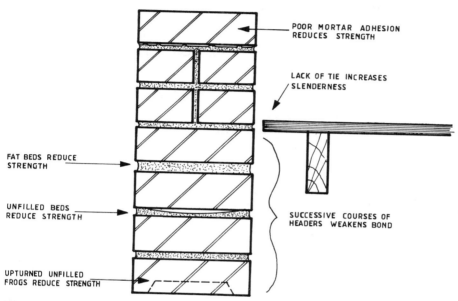

Figure 3.10 *Masonry strength reducers*

Mortar strength is not a preoccupation of many investigations but, as with slenderness, new or abnormal loading can expose weakness. Even then, it is not usually the average mortar strength which causes problems but a local weakness due to poor workmanship. Mixing mortar is not an unskilled job. If carried out carelessly, patches of walls may be built with mortar of negligible cement content, leaving them vulnerable to tensile stress which may only occur during accidents. Another fault which is more likely to lead to defects than merely weak mortar is poor adhesion between the mortar and the masonry units. This occurs most often with porous units which, if laid dry, especially in warm weather, will rapidly absorb water from the surface of the fresh mortar. The mortar is thereby rendered harsh and non-plastic, and fails to adhere to the units. In these circumstances, the bed joints have no tensile strength. At the opposite extreme, dense impermeable bricks, with low suction, may fail to adhere to a lean dry mortar, and again there is poor adhesion, leaving the bed joint weak in tension.

If bed joints are excessively wide there could be a reduction in the wall strength of up to roughly 25 per cent. Badly filled bed joints can have a similar effect, but the quality of perpends is less important.

Stretcher bond is probably the strongest bond in brickwork. Any other bond in brick, block or stone, where the perpends are not well staggered, can reduce the strength of the wall. The typical rough guide for strength reduction due to a weak bond is about 25 per cent.

The strength of the mortar itself, when it is free from faults, has little influence on the typically lightly stressed walls of most traditional buildings. For Ordinary Portland Cement, the range is perhaps 25 per cent between strongest and weakest, and this is much less than the strength range of brick, block or stone. The mortar strength range is wider for highly stressed masonry, and for lime mortar, but even in these circumstances damage due to mortar being much weaker than the units is very rare.

The different effects of unit strength, wall slenderness, mortar quality, adhesion between mortar and masonry, bed thickness and masonry bond are cumulative. A robust brick wall in strong mortar might be virtually as strong as its individual units, whereas rubble stonework in lime mortar might have only a third the strength of its weaker stone, even if it has no slenderness problems.

But the problem of reduced compressive strength should not be over emphasized. In established buildings, it is seldom a real worry. Tensile damage and potential instability are the two major preoccupations.

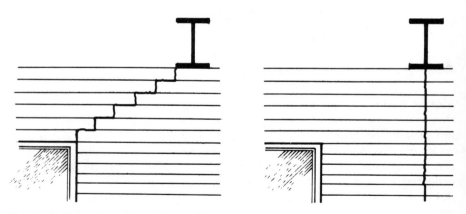

Figure 3.11   *Damage at concentrated load*

Concentrated loads

Masonry cracking can occur beneath a concentrated load for one of two reasons: either the load represents a restraint, so that any strain that the wall is undergoing, whether from thermal movement or subsidence or whatever, is likely to focus at that point; or the load causes a bearing failure by overstressing the masonry. The alternatives are shown on Figure 3.11. In the first case (restraint) the damage often occurs to one side of the load, whereas in the second (overstressing) it nearly always occurs beneath it. The effect of restraint is discussed again in chapter 4.

Immediately beneath a concentrated load, masonry is in triaxial compression, but a short distance below that zone there is a small ellipse of tension. Typically, maximum tension occurs at a distance beneath the load roughly equal to the width of the load itself. This is where failure develops. If maximum tension exceeds the capacity of the masonry, a crack will form at that level. It then tends to propagate vertically, even if it is near the end of the wall or the edge of an opening, but of course minor effects, such as variations in mortar strength or longitudinal strain, can occasionally induce the crack to turn horizontally or diagonally.

Damage caused by overstress is not very common. If the damage is old and the load has not significantly increased since the damage occurred, it simply represents stress release which is seldom dangerous and is usually easy to repair by stitching in stronger units.

Alterations

Probably the most frequently observed alteration is the removal of the ground

Figure 3.12 *Damage caused by inserting opening*

floor front wall to form a shop front. When this is not properly done the consequences are obvious (Figure 3.12). There are two dangers: the first floor and storey above have to be adequately propped while the ground floor wall is removed, and then they have to be tightly pinned to the new supporting beam (Figure 3.13) – otherwise movement and damage are inevitable; second, it is not always realized by designers that even beams which are designed within current British Standard limits can still deflect enough to damage existing walls. Damage caused by such small movement is nearly always cosmetic and non-progressive, but it can cause a little panic.

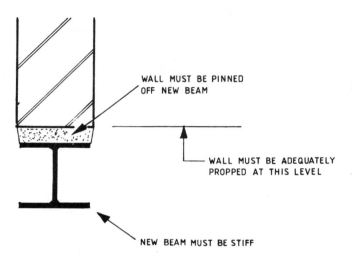

Figure 3.13   *Precautions with new support*

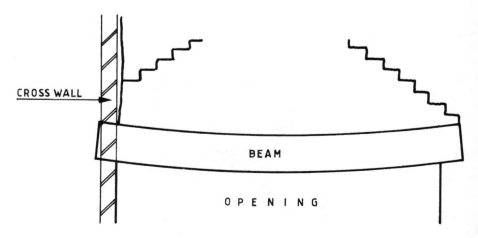

Figure 3.14   *Damage to poorly supported masonry*

If the movement, whatever its cause, is more than trivial, the wall may flex sufficiently to not only crack (Figure 3.14) but to disrupt its bond with cross walls. Lost bond ought to be restored, especially if the wall is not well tied at floor and roof levels.

Similar alterations may have been made to internal walls, but they are not as easily spotted because buildings can only be viewed internally a storey at a time, so indoor support is not necessarily conspicuous by its absence. To add to the difficulties of inspection, damage may have been covered, without being repaired, during redecoration.

It is not unknown for a complete load bearing storey to be removed without any compensating support. It is often difficult to imagine, when inspecting such abuse, how collapse has been averted, but it is important to find out because stability may be precarious; a further slight alteration may not be accommodated.

Well-built masonry walls are capable of arching across loss of support. Stable and undamaged walls have been found to be completely without support for a distance of several metres. This superficially satisfactory but very sensitive arrangement is easily destroyed by the insertion of a door.

Some walls were built off floorboards at each level, even though they were intended to act as vertically continuous load-bearing partitions. If they lose support, the floor joists, assisted sometimes by the floorboards acting as a compression flange, may help in resisting load, although not always without serious distortion.

Vanishing chimneys are a menace to surveyors. The stack is sometimes removed from one storey but left in place in the storey or roof above. It may have been given support at its new base but that is often difficult to prove. It may instead be relying on its ability to corbel from a party wall, assisted by some accidental propping by floor joists, and this precarious stability might be sustained for many years until destroyed by some small and apparently non-structural act.

Stud walls may have the ability to act as trusses, if they lose support, with their coverings performing as diagonal ties. Again, the arrangement may be sensitive to minor change. It is not well enough known that some stud walls were actually designed as trusses and were intended to span between cross walls or piers. These elements never had support, but they are all the more vulnerable to alteration which is almost bound to cut through one or more of their individual flanges, ties or struts.

Abused trusses can often be secretly reframed. Most other cases of gross abuse by alteration need more substantial attention.

Lintels

A lot of external wall damage occurs at lintels and if appraisal is limited to a visual inspection it is difficult to decide whether the fault lies with the lintel itself, or the wall, or the wall's foundations.

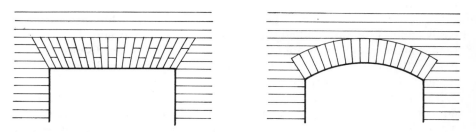

Figure 3.15 *Arch lintels*

Two traditional lintels are vulnerable: the shallow arch and the flat arch (Figure 3.15). Both are required to transfer small compression forces across their vertical (or near vertical) masonry joints. That is not the problem. The problem is that, except with steep arches, there are shear forces parallel to the joints which may tend to cause slumping (Figure 3.16) or less obvious distortion, leading to damage of the brickwork above. These shear forces are always present. They are small and harmless until movement is mobilized by normal wear and tear of the mortar in the joints or by very slight spread of the brickwork beside the opening. The latter may be caused either by the buttressing force itself or by foundation movement, or by thermal expansion of the wall (Figure 3.17).

Figure 3.16 *Slumped lintel*

The concrete boot lintel was briefly popular in the mid twentieth century. It had a tendency to rotate forwards because its outer ledge, while supporting load, was not itself supported, and the loading was therefore not in line with the bearing (Figure 3.18). Soft packing at bearings sometimes exacerbated this eccentricity. The result was bulging and cracking of the panel above, seldom severe but always unsightly.

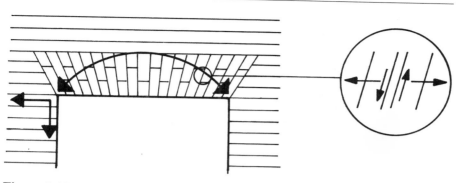

Figure 3.17 *Effect of movement*

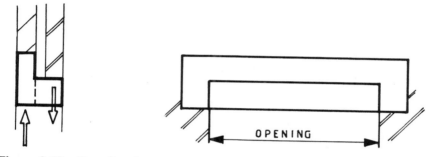

Figure 3.18 *Boot lintel*

A similar problem is sometimes seen with steel lintels which have a thin shelf supporting the external leaf. The shelf is in turn supported by a stiff section which does most of the work, spanning across the inner leaf. The shelf is stiff enough not to deflect measurably itself, but the brick leaf it supports can rotate if it overhangs by more than a third of its thickness, or if its bedding mortar is poor and allows consolidation. (Occasionally, the mortar bed is made wider at opening head levels in an effort to revert to brick gauge, and a fat bed on a steel surface is not ideal, especially if the mortar is wet or lean.) As with boot lintels, the problem is rarely more than cosmetic, but it is common enough to deserve a mention for the purpose of distinguishing it from potentially more serious causes of damage.

Floors

Floors are abused as often as walls, and unfortunately they have lower reserves of strength. Notching joists for services is the favourite form of abuse. Notching and drilling outside the zones illustrated in Figure 3.19 will reduce the floor's strength and stiffness and may cause, or add to, any problems with deflection. The probability of damage due to future imposed loading may be checked by structural calculation. Joists deeper than 250mm, and joists supporting concentrated loads, cannot be fitted to any standard safe notch pattern, and an individual calculation should be made.

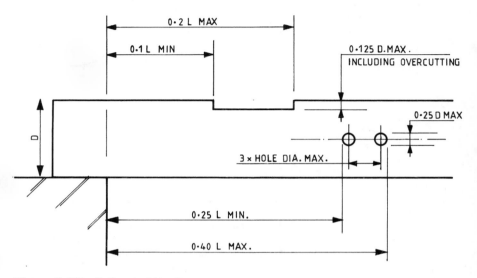

Figure 3.19   *Safe notching limits*

Building heavy partitions off floorboards is another common abuse (Figure 3.20). Not until the 1970s did it become common practice to design supports for partitions. Before then, even brick walls were lucky to get one extra joist beneath them.

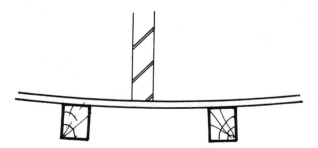

Figure 3.20   *Overloaded joists*

Principal beams in mediaeval buildings may be performing two important functions: carrying a large proportion of the total roof (or floor) loading; and forming a tie across the building. If they are cut to insert stairs or standard-height doors, the whole building may suffer. Some characteristic timber-frame problems are discussed in Chapter 15.

Timber floors which are undersized or weakened will creep to abnormal deflections. In theory, they may be incapable of supporting standard imposed loading, but in practice the actual loading in houses and commercial buildings is nearly always lower than the values required for design by British Standard. In prestigious buildings, abnormal deflection is often disguised by relevelling the surface and hanging new ceiling joists (Figure 3.21), without supplying any strengthening or stiffening.

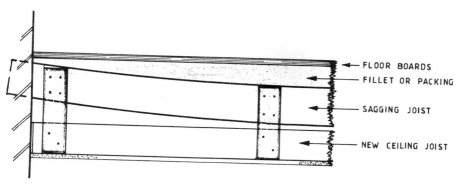

Figure 3.21 *Disguised floor distortion*

Warehouses and other heavily loaded buildings may be found to have steel-plated timber floors. Concrete, filler joist and jack arch floors are also common. Appraisal of their past performance is simple, and they are usually found to be satisfactory. Future performance under change of load is sometimes difficult to determine without cutting trial holes or load testing.

Vibration

Vibration gets a bad press because the threshold of human discomfort is well below the threshold of structural discomfort. The majority of public complaints are genuine, understandable and misguided. Naturally, people make a tour of inspection when they think that their home or office has been shaken, and they are quite likely to find the evidence they are looking for, usually in the form of minor plaster cracking which is not in fact new but had previously escaped notice.

If windows crack, the evidence is more alarming. In most cases vibration, if it was the cause, was only the last straw. Glass is often compressed, and indeed often fails, as a result of its own expansion, the swelling of its wooden frame (or rusting of its metal frame), over-tight glazing sprigs, distortion from thermal or foundation movement and of course impact. Even more rarely, masonry which was on the brink of cracking due to stresses from other causes may succumb during vibration. Continuing vibration then has little effect.

It is possible that wind and ground vibrations may accelerate the long-term decay of materials, masonry in particular, but this is not a theory which is easily, or in many cases usefully, tested.

Returning to immediate effects: vibration may be air-borne or ground-borne. The former causes doors and windows to rattle but can do nothing to healthy buildings. The latter can cause the ground to densify (see Chapter 6), although that, too, is a rare cause of damage, and it can cause structural elements to resonate. Ground-borne vibration is usually felt by occupants through the floors, because their natural frequency is closer than walls to most types of vibration.

Road traffic does not generate enough energy in acceleration and deceleration to cause any serious discomfort, but potholes create high vertical energy. Most traffic-induced vibration damage is the result of bad road surfaces.

Particles excited by vibration accelerate from their static position, reaching a peak velocity and then displacement before returning to their original position and going through further cycles of movement until the energy decays or is damped. Table 3.2 gives a very rough idea of the relationship between human perception and structural danger. A full description of, or enquiry into, potential vibration damage should take all the other characteristics into account as well.

Table 3.2   *Vibration: human and structural response*

PEAK PARTICLE VELOCITY mm/sec.	EFFECT.
0.3	THRESHOLD OF PERCEPTION: MAY CAUSE ANNOYANCE IN RURAL AREAS IF UNEXPECTED.
2	VERY POOR QUALITY DECORATION (e.g. AGED LATH AND PLASTER) MIGHT BE DAMAGED.
2.5	MAY CAUSE ANNOYANCE IN AN URBAN ENVIRONMENT.
5	UNPLEASANT TO OCCUPANTS: PLASTER DAMAGE.
10	EXTREMELY UNPLEASANT: MINOR STRUCTURAL DAMAGE POSSIBLE.

A deteriorating road surface would introduce perceptible vibrations, which would be unexpected, and would quickly lead to annoyance and complaints if the deterioration continued through break-up by frost or traffic. Irregularities of 20mm can cause peak particle velocities of 5mm/sec. in the immediate vicinity.

The effect of tracked vehicles has been monitored on occasions and it is generally accepted that no damage occurs to properties 15m or more away from the source. Trains create larger ground-borne vibrations in their immediate vicinity and they lead to more complaints by building owners and occupants, but known cases of damage are rare. Continuous rail tracks are less likely to cause discomfort from trains than jointed ones.

Piledriving causes horizontal and vertical shock waves which decay quickly in soft ground but which can be refracted or reflected in firm ground. For example, a hard level underground stratum can reflect the shock back to the surface with sufficient energy to cause a noticeable effect on buildings 100m or so away. As with traffic vibration, there is a gulf between the threshold of anxiety and the threshold of damage. The potential damage can be reduced by using lower energy or by drilling a pilot hole from the ground surface so that the actual driving only starts at a certain distance below ground level, thus lengthening the path taken by the direct waves. There are alternative methods of piling by which the piles are installed by vibrating them into the ground at special frequencies which do not cause resonance.

Dancing can cause floor resonance, which is uncomfortable and possibly dangerous if it leads to large deflections. The risk of damage or unacceptable floor deflection can be arithmetically assessed by a structural engineer. The calculation is not exact and, if necessary, a dynamic test can be conducted, although in many cases the money would be better spent in carrying out a degree of stiffening which would make the floor safe beyond doubt.

Chapter 4

CAUSES OF DAMAGE: SHRINKAGE AND EXPANSION

The purpose of this chapter is to outline the effects of volume changes, independent of loads and other hazards.

Moisture content and temperature

Shrinkage and expansion arise from changes in moisture content and temperature. These cause volume changes which would be harmless if they could take place freely, but free movement can only occur in materials isolated from their surroundings, a condition to be avoided with buildings. Movement joints achieve partial separation but never isolation – a necessary distinction, and one reason why they are difficult to design well. Table 4.1 lists the free movement of some building materials.

In practice there is a compromise between the element wishing to change shape without stress and its surrounding elements which restrain its movement and impose stress. One way to test the possibility of moisture or thermal movement having caused the damage is to model this compromise; imagine first the free movement; then identify the restraint (or restraints); then consider the effect of the restraint.

Shrinkage

An example of shrinkage is shown in Figure 4.1. A wall is built to first-floor

Table 4.1   *Free movement*

Youngs modulus kN/mm²	Material	Permanent Movements		Temporary movements	
		Drying shrinkage %	Moisture expansion%	Moisture movement %	Thermal movement $\times 10^{-6}$ per C°
4 to 26	Clay bricks	nil	0.02 to 0.06	0.02	5 to 8
14 to 28	Calcium silicate bricks	0.01 to 0.04	—	0.03 to 0.06	10 to 13
10 to 25	Dense concrete blocks	0.02 to 0.06	—	0.02 to 0.04	6 to 12
4 to 16	Lightweight aggregate (autoclaved) blocks	0.02 to 0.06	—	0.03 to 0.06	8 to 12
3 to 8	Aerated (autoclaved) blocks	0.05 to 0.09	—	0.02 to 0.03	8
20 to 35	Mortar	0.04 to 0.10	—	0.03 to 0.06	10 to 13
20 to 60	Granite	—	—	—	8 to 10
10 to 80	Limestone	—	—	0.004 to 0.013	3 to 8
3 to 80	Sandstone	—	—	0.025 to 0.070	7 to 10

(Permanent drying shrinkage bracket note: *Occasionally higher if units are built in while still green or saturated.*)

(Temporary moisture movement bracket note: *Assumes variation from dry to saturated*)

(Thermal movement bracket note: *Typical temperature variation (UK): dark masonry 60°C, light masonry 50°C; internal 25°C, if uninhabited 40°C*)

| 5.5 to 12.5 | Softwood | In wood, moisture movement is approximately reversible, but in new buildings initial shrinkage of softwood can be regarded as permanent, causing typical movements of 3% tangential, 1½% radial, 0% longitudinal. If the timber was supplied unusually wet or if internal conditions are unusually dry, shrinkage may double. Exceptionally dry conditions may force locally exceptional shrinkage | | 0.6 to 2.6 tangential / 0.45 to 2.0 radial / Nil longitudinal | 4 to 6 with grain / 30 to 70 across grain |
| 7 to 21 | Hardwood | | | 0.8 to 4.0 tangential / 0.5 to 2.5 radial / Nil longitudinal | 4 to 6 with grain / 30 to 70 across grain |

(Wood temporary moisture bracket note: *Assumes variation from 90% RH to 60% RH*)

Free movement:

For shrinkage & moisture movement   Change of size = factor × original size

For thermal movement   Change of size = Factor × temperature range × original size

(Factors as tabulated above)

Actual movement = Free movement — Restraint

Restraint reduces movement and introduces stress. It may act both in line with the movement and eccentrically, and it may be more effective in one direction than the other

Damage to element undergoing shrinkage = free shortening — (actual shortening — tensile capacity)

level in brickwork. It continues above in lightweight concrete blockwork. (If exposed, the blockwork is likely to be rendered, but that would not significantly affect its performance.)

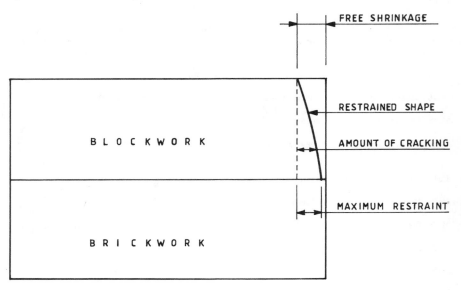

Figure 4.1   *Shrinkage*

Left on its own, the blockwork would shrink linearly. But it is bonded along its lower surface to brickwork which is stiff and does not shrink. The brickwork permits the blockwork a certain amount of shrinkage, accepting a compressive load in the process, but most is prevented, and the blockwork wall is in effect stretched from the length it prefers (free shrinkage) close to the length the brickwork prefers (no change). So the blockwork experiences tension. Blockwork is not strong in tension, and the amount of stretch is roughly the measure of expected cracking. This may occur either as a single vertical tapering crack or as a number of cracks whose accumulative width would be about the same.

The example is over simplified. The blockwork would be restrained not only by the brickwork. It would be restrained vertically at either end as well as, to a lesser degree, along its top edge. These additional restraints complicate the pattern of movement and damage. Furthermore, the blockwork can undergo 0.05–0.1 per cent tensile strain before cracking, so that total crack width is slightly less than free movement minus restraint.

It is possible to make a rigorous analysis based on relative stiffness, but exact calculation is not possible. Most cases can be judged by the simplified model, choosing the major restraint, and if the damage follows a logical pattern without exceeding the degree that would be expected of the material, then shrinkage remains a possibility.

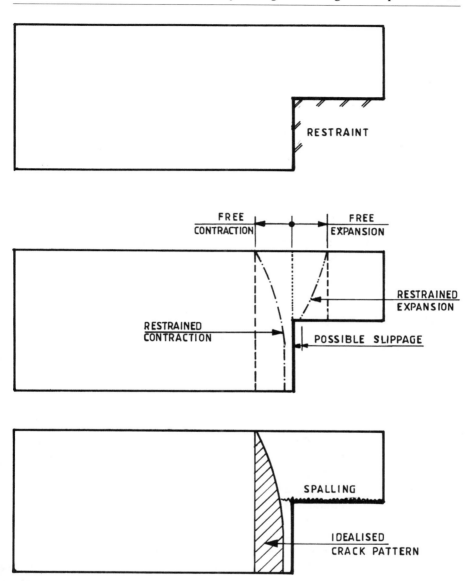

Figure 4.2   *Thermal movement*

Reversible temperature movement

A similar model can be made for reversible temperature movement. The strength of the restraint may not be quite the same in both directions, and the starting point would depend on temperature during construction, so a diagrammatic study would be even more of a simplification.

Figure 4.2 shows a long external wall restrained towards one end, but only at its lower level, so that the restraint acts as a stiff buttress. There are two phases to consider: contraction (or shrinkage); and expansion. Shrinkage can be judged in a similar way to the previous example, with free movement permitted at the top edge but largely prevented below mid-height. This encourages tapered cracking (ignoring for the sake of simplicity any tensile capacity in the masonry, and the effect of other restraints or weaknesses). Expansion also occurs freely at the top edge. It occurs not at all below mid-height (assuming this time for the sake of simplicity that the restraint is infinitely stiff). Restrained expansion causes compression which masonry accepts without damage, so this phase theoretically causes no cracking. In practice, slippage may occur close to the sharp transition at the top of the restraint. This may appear as spalling along the bed course; in addition perpends may be shunted open close to the top corner of the restraint.

Actual damage will not inevitably form at the face of the restraint, nor will it normally take a purely vertical route. Its pattern will be influenced by the usual unknowable variations in material properties.

Material behaviour

Drying shrinkage affects both blockwork and calcium silicate brickwork. In both cases, cracking is attracted to the restraints causing it, and to openings which locally increase the tensile stress in the stretched wall. The damage is usually fully developed within a year.

Abnormal shrinkage can, however, prolong and exaggerate the damage, and this most often occurs if the blocks or bricks are used wet from unprotected stacks. Alternatively, building work might be interrupted, leaving the carcass open to wet weather for longer than usual. In either case, the high moisture content at the time of construction means that subsequent moisture content reduction is greater than normal, and so is the shrinkage. The use of concrete blocks very fresh from manufacture also increases shrinkage.

Calcium silicate bricks are sensitive to weather conditions, particularly rain, during construction, and it has been noticed that south and west elevations are at greater risk than north and east. Detailing has more of an influence than with other masonry materials. Long panels are more likely to crack than short panels of equal area, and this risk increases sharply when the length to height ratio exceeds three.

The shrinkage of timber depends not only on its moisture loss, but on which part of the tree it came from (Figure 4.3), tangential shrinkage being greater than radial. In the longitudinal direction, shrinkage is usually negligible. The initial moisture content of timber is typically 18 per cent during construction, but timber stacked without protection or built in and left exposed in uncompleted buildings during wet weather can reach a moisture content of 24 per cent or locally even higher. When the building has dried out, the moisture content would typically fall to about 12 per cent, but it would be less in warm dry spaces such as airing cupboards, and it could be locally much less near central heating pipes. Very roughly, tangential shrinkage is one third of moisture change, in this range. Radial shrinkage is roughly half the tangential.

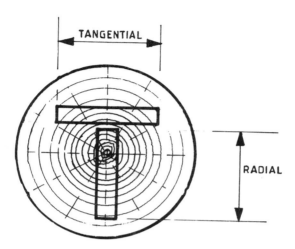

Figure 4.3   *Timber origins*

Timber shrinkage may remove support from a partition. The partition may then crack in a typical pattern (Figure 4.4), which would be virtually indistinguishable by visual inspection from damage caused by deflection under load. For this reason, shrinkage is often mistaken by owners and occupants for structural failure. The difference is not always obvious to the professional, either. Shrinkage occurs early and is non-progressive, and it is considerably the more common problem in new buildings. Over-deflection can also cause early damage, but it is likely to have a creep component which, together with the effect of short-term loading, is likely to cause at least some mild progression. A distortion survey (Chapter 10) can detect gross deflection under load, provided this is not masked by large inbuilt variations. If it is, it will be necessary to remove coverings and make a close inspection in order to distinguish between shrinkage and deflection. Shrinkage leaves no mark, but over-deflected floors sometimes (by no means always) exhibit distress in the more highly stressed areas. Structural calculation would provide a useful estimate of deflection. Its theoretical consequence can then be compared with actual damage. Calculation, to be useful, must be based on a realistic assessment of the quality of the timber and applied loading, and not on numbers taken from a design code. (If the future capacity of the floor is needed, then standards would of course be consulted, but timber properties should still be based on what is there.)

A change of use, or even a change of occupancy, can dry a building more than previously and cause a regeneration of drying shrinkage. The timing can then surprise everyone, and a structural defect is even more likely to be assumed.

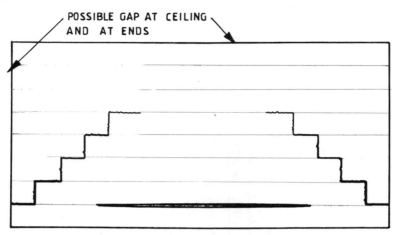

POSSIBLE GAP AT CEILING
AND AT ENDS

Figure 4.4 *Partition damaged by loss of support.*

Mediaeval timber frames were built of large unseasoned sections restrained by their own strong connections, and this is one reason for their present crazy shapes – not always the only reason, alas.

Modern timber frame also shrinks and, during construction, allowance ought to be made for this at eaves and verges. If it is neglected, the timber frame may open slightly at panel edges. Alternatively or in addition the brick skin may bow due to eccentric compression; window sills, particularly within the upper storey, may demonstrate the movement by tilting inwards. The problem is not common and is hardly ever more than cosmetic.

Thermal movement affects all materials. Timber has tensile strength and distorts without cracking. As already observed, masonry is most likely to crack when it is restrained against contracting. South facing walls and dark materials move the most.

Clay brickwork, alone among masonry materials, undergoes irreversible expansion which occurs as the brick absorbs moisture vapour. The expansion takes place vertically as well as longitudinally. It first came to general notice as a result of damage caused to frames by vertical expansion of brickwork used fresh from the kiln during a brick shortage. If bricks are not used for a few days after firing, nearly half the movement occurs harmlessly. The remaining proportion is less likely to cause damage, not only because there is less of it but because it takes place much more slowly, so that the forces it generates are partly dissipated by stress relaxation. The initial movement is not significantly accelerated by wetting the bricks.

Since irreversible moisture movement is, after the first few days, slow and one way (expansive), fairly low restraining forces are sufficient to prevent its taking place altogether. Moreover, any damage caused by the restraining action will usually occur to the restraining element rather than the brickwork itself, since the latter would be subject to compression. (If the restraint is eccentric, of course, there will be a tendency to bow, resisted by the brickwork's bending stiffness.)

Typical signs of irreversible moisture movement are almost restricted to: oversailing of the damp proof course, particularly of bungalows; similar slippage of parapets and balconies; and slight damage of return walls and other weak restraints to long lengths of expanding brick. The last type is also characteristic of reversible thermal movement, and the two effects can be mildly cumulative. Bricks made from Weald Clay appear to suffer greater irreversible movement than other types.

In clay brickwork, damage due to reversible movement can be expected in walls without movement joints which are 15m long or longer. In some cases, walls only 10m long have been damaged. Calcium silicate bricks can be expected to crack in 9m walls and may crack in only 5m walls, although in their case the original cause is usually drying shrinkage rather than thermal movement, Stone masonry hardly shrinks but it expands as much as typical brickwork. The consequences are often witnessed on long terraces without joints, but cracking is generally not on the same scale as calculated movement, whereas with brickwork it can be. This may be partly because stone is more massive and more difficult to restrain. Its greater thickness also means that the temperature difference between outside and inside is greater, with therefore, potentially less differential movement between external walls and their internal restraints such as party walls. There may be differential expansion between mineral components of the stone itself, sufficient to cause widespread but tiny surface cracking, which can look more like weathering than thermal damage.

Moisture variations in masonry cause the same types of movement, but on a smaller scale than temperature. Moisture increase causes expansion. For most of the time moisture movement opposes temperature movement, moisture evaporating as temperature rises, so that the maximum range of thermal/moisture movement is usually slightly less than the full thermal range.

Thermal and moisture movements are cyclical. In theory, so is the damage. In practice it is sometimes mildly progressive. This is not inevitable but it can occur if restraint is modified after damage has appeared or if it varies at different times throughout the cycle. The crack itself might offer resistance to closure as its alignment varies slightly from one cycle to another, or as grit clogs it. This tendency to be progressive is rarely a problem in itself, but it can lead to mistaken diagnosis.

In the examples chosen to illustrate shrinkage and expansion (Figures 4.1 and 4.2), the elements undergoing the movement were shown to suffer the damage. Their restraints, though accepting some stress, remained intact. There are circumstances when the opposite happens. Perhaps the best known is the ubiquitous return wall (Figure 4.5) rotated by the expansion of the main walls. A long or weak return wall will often form a shear crack roughly in line with the inside face of the expanding/contracting wall. A shorter or stronger wall is more likely to induce a crack at the end of the main walls.

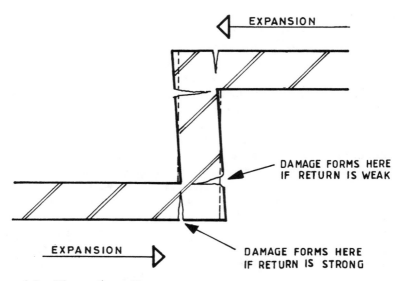

Figure 4.5   *Thermal cracking*

The expansion of flat or mono-pitched roofs can apply a force at right angles to the supporting walls (Figure 4.6), which offer token restraint before failing in shear. Damage occurs at or near roof level. The force is intermittent and sudden, and walls do not find it easy to give way gracefully. Furthermore, the brickwork does not always return with the roof as it goes through its shrinkage cycle, so there is mild progression. Expansion may also become more extreme over the years if the roof's reflective chippings are lost, allowing an increase in temperature variation.

Timber and concrete expand by similar amounts but the latter is more difficult to restrain and is more likely to cause damage, especially if it is not insulated and has no friction break at the top of supporting walls.

Movements of 25mm have been observed at the edges of 20m wide roofs. These far exceed what would be expected from a single cycle, and must represent many cycles of stick and slip. In most cases, damage is not more than cosmetic.

Concrete floor shrinkage

Concrete floors shrink. As with masonry materials, the movement is short lived and irreversible. The symptoms are quite different from timber shrinkage, because concrete movement is mainly longitudinal, whereas timber's is sectional. Bearings beneath concrete floors may be pulled inwards, creating the opposite effect to that shown in Figure 4.6. If the bearings coincide with natural weaknesses within the structure, horizontal bending and cracking may occur in the supporting walls, and vertical cracking may develop in walls bonded at right angles to them.

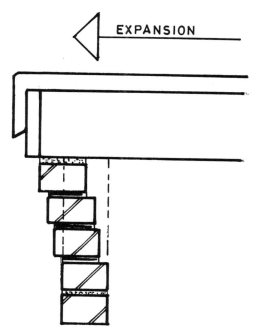

Figure 4.6   *Roof expansion*

Precast concrete floors will have gone through at least part of their shrinkage before being placed. If the precast units are prestressed, rather than merely reinforced, they may continue to creep due to stresses imposed by the prestressing force (or sometimes its relaxation). Creep would prolong the effect of shrinkage, although damage is seldom more than slight. In the case of prestressed beam and block floors, the creep is seen most often at ceiling level, in the form of a tearing along the line between beam and block.

In situ concrete, of course, suffers all its shrinkage in place, and damage can be spectacular (although rarely severe) when floors are cast in long lengths without joints at intermediate supports.

To summarize the discussion on shrinkage and expansion: all materials experience a characteristic range of movement; buildings undergo continuous small changes of shape and stress in response to these individual movements. The boundaries of acceptable movement are well established, but not always well accommodated. It is not purely a design problem. Some permanent movements – shrinkage of lightweight concrete blocks, for example – are difficult to control, and it could be argued that temporary damage is preferable to providing joints at inconvenient positions.

Movement due to shrinkage or expansion is the greatest single cause of slight damage to new buildings. Occasionally the movement is severe enough to cause serviceability problems, and the two most common circumstances are shrinkage caused by materials being used in too wet a condition, and expansion caused by large external surface areas having no movement joints, or badly detailed joints.

The damage is caused by the consequences of this movement: restraining forces are set up or support is removed from partitions. These consequences can develop in unexpected ways and are not always recognized. For example, the imaginary case of differential shrinkage and expansion shown on Figure 4.7 could lead to: bowing of the external leaf of the wall; a horizontal crack on the inside skin, close to ceiling level; or a rotation of the top of the wall. Any of those symptoms could be mistaken for structural movement, unless investigation is methodical.

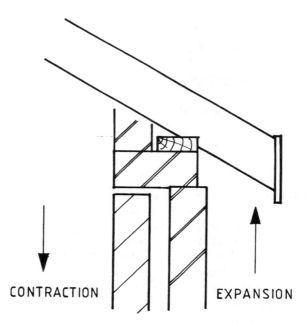

CONTRACTION   EXPANSION

Figure 4.7   *Differential volume change*

Because slight damage from shrinkage and expansion is so widespread, investigators must be able to distinguish these movements from the early stages of more serious structural problems, and this is often not possible from a visual inspection alone. The need to take evidence from different viewpoints is discussed in other chapters.

Chapter 5

CAUSES OF DAMAGE:
DETERIORATION

The purpose of this chapter is to outline the common causes of structural damage which arise from wear and tear or from the long-term consequence of inappropriate materials.

Timber decay

There is a potential for rot when the moisture content of timber rises above 20 per cent. The first consequence is a weakening of the timber caused by a gradual breakdown of the fibres. This leads to fungal attack which causes further weakening. It is not a rapid process; only a persistently high moisture content will lead to rot. Insects make better progress in wood which has partly broken down, so conditions which encourage rot will also encourage infestation.

The source of unwanted moisture is generally damp penetration. Condensation is responsible for a minority of cases, and undetected leakage for an occasional one. Lack of ventilation is a great encourager of dry rot which, although it is less common than wet rot, is able to thrive at lower moisture contents and, once established, can transmit moisture to new timber so as to assist the spread of rot.

The most common attacker of softwoods in the UK is the common furniture beetle. Wood boring weevils also attack softwood but only when it is so wet or decayed that it is of little structural value anyway. The house longhorn beetle infests softwood but is geographically restricted in the UK to Surrey and adjacent counties. Under current building regulations, new timber should be treated to deter the spread of this insect. Details of suspected outbreaks should be reported to the Building Research Establishment's Timber and Protection Division which maintains records of infestations in the UK.

The only common serious attacker of hardwoods in the UK is the death-watch beetle, which is happiest in oak but can infest other species, even, very occasionally, softwoods. Damp is necessary for its establishment, although the attack may then continue despite subsequent drying out. Both rot and infestation favour sapwood but can be encouraged to move onto heartwood in very damp conditions.

To the general practitioner, rot and infestation can both be elusive because the most spectacular symptoms, fruit bodies and adult insects, are seldom on display. Outbreaks enjoy covered and inaccessible areas, and when detected are easy to confuse with harmless moulds and insects.

Structural appraisal has to take into account not only the damage done so far but whatever damage is to come, and that in turn depends on the proposed treatment. Unless infestation control kills larvae as well as emerging insects and eggs, further deterioration must be considered in the structural appraisal, as the larvae live for several years inside the wood without surfacing.

Preservatives are not a long term cure for rot. Removal of the damp conditions which allowed it to develop in the first place is an essential part of the treatment, and further deterioration is possible until the timber moisture content has been reduced to 20 per cent or so. At best, preservatives keep rot at bay during this drying out period. Timber which is highly stressed may need support while it is still wet, because it is not only weakened by high moisture content, but is liable to suffer large immediate and creep deflections. Provided the treatment is assured and allowances made for any short term weakness and deterioration while infestation or rot continue, an assessment can then be made of the strength of the timber.

The detection of rot and infestation is particularly important with mediaeval buildings. They have survived most other hazards, and decay is their greatest current danger. The durability of oak sole plates set in the ground, or maybe on stone but without a damp proof course, is remarkable, but not infinite. The point is eventually reached when sole plate deterioration is serious enough to undermine the whole building. Studs connected into rotting sole plates are always affected because moisture finds it easier to penetrate end grain than cross grain.

Location of rot and infestation

Since damp penetration is its main cause, rot is found in the areas most vulnerable to damp. Faulty rainwater goods are the most common source of entry. Problems start at the top, where some of the rainwater can miss the gutter if the sarking is unsupported or if the gutter is not well placed to receive the run-off from the roof covering. Penetration can also occur through leakage, blockage or under-capacity of gutters, and at broken hoppers or deteriorated downpipes, particularly where the spillage can run along brackets and right through the wall by way of eroded mortar joints. Other vulnerable areas include damaged flashings, badly detailed projections and failed or missing damp proof courses.

These potential locations are often easier to detect externally. Internally, afflicted areas may be covered or difficult to visit. The timber which is most at risk is obviously that which is closest to areas of potential damp penetration, particularly members which greet it end grain on.

In large built-in timbers, the interior of the timber section may be more favourable to insect attack than the surface layers, particularly at locations which are now dry but have previously been damp. Timbers built into solid walls may suffer rot even though there is no apparent damp penetration. Walls which are exposed or whose mortar joints are porous or perished create the greatest risk, and problems can be expected in buildings which have not been well maintained. External walls may incorporate timber backing lintels or bands of timber (Figure 5.1) which are also vulnerable to external exposure.

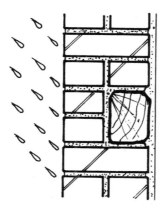

Figure 5.1   *Vulnerable timber*

Renovation may cause an increase in condensation within the roof space which, if serious, can cause rot and encourage infestation. Examples of, in this respect, unfortunate renovations are the removal of fireplaces and installation of double glazing (reducing natural ventilation), the installation of additional bathrooms or kitchen when converting to flats (increasing humidity) and the provision of roof insulation (also increasing humidity by decreasing the winter temperature in the roof space).

Provision of insulation may also obstruct eaves ventilation which would in turn encourage condensation, especially within low-pitched roofs. If the roof has ridge or gable ventilation, this may give the impression that the roof space is still ventilated but, without the cross flow that eaves ventilation provides, ridge or gable ventilation may do more harm than good by sucking more of the humid air straight into the roof space from the floor below than would otherwise trickle through.

Deterioration of metal connectors, hangers or clamps can occur in conditions which promote rot, and they can also be at risk from tannic acid in oak or certain preservatives and fire retardants.

Masonry decay

The decay of masonry walls can also be insidious for the same reason: the cause is generally hidden. But unlike timber, it is not easy to reveal by uncovering vulnerable spots. Unless an extremely thorough inspection is justified, as might be the case if substantial refurbishment threatens to increase stresses in walls, we have to wait for symptoms to become apparent.

Internal walls were often built ahead of external walls, and not bonded into them. This may leave external walls more slender than they appear and thereby more vulnerable to damage than might be expected. Conversely, of course, there is opportunity to reduce slenderness and improve strength and stability at reasonable cost.

Sometimes the cross walls, and even the external flank walls, were built of low quality studwork, and seldom tied to the masonry at junctions. Again the consequence is a hidden weakness which can be simply cured, provided the materials themselves have endured.

Masonry cross walls, and other internal walls, were often built to lower standards using poorer quality material, such as underfired bricks. Such walls may have consolidated in the past and will have been readily damaged if burdened with even modest alteration.

The same poor quality material was sometimes used in the internal skin of external walls, hidden behind facing brickwork or ashlar. This has sometimes led to distortion as the internal skin has shortened under load, causing bowing of the outer (Figure 5.2). In the long term the internal skin may also have suffered deterioration caused, for example, by penetrating damp eroding its mortar or rotting the bands of timber reinforcement which these walls sometimes contain (Figure 5.1). Again, the result has been shortening of the internal skin and bowing of the outer.

Frost damage eats into masonry by the action of absorbed water freezing and repeatedly splitting off the face of the unit. Surfaces which are regularly soaked are most likely to be damaged. Earth retaining walls of porous masonry with no damp proof membrane are particularly vulnerable. So are water-collecting projections and ledges, as well as masonry which is accidentally soaked by faulty rainwater goods or traffic splashing. Water from melting snow has least chance of evaporating before the next freeze cycle, and most chance of doing damage. Parapets, chimneys and walls which trap snow (Figure 3.3) will attract this particular risk. In one case, a chimney was built of frost resistant bricks above the roof line but of frost susceptible bricks below, and frost damage within the roof space became serious enough to cause instability. The damage had been caused by water percolating downwards past faulty flashings and then freezing within the roof space.

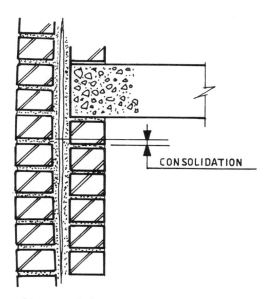

Figure 5.2 *Inner skin consolidation*

It is the frequency of saturation, rather than the frequency of low temperature, which determines the risk of frost damage, and the areas of the UK which are most exposed to driving rain are therefore the most vulnerable.

Frost resistance cannot be measured by a single property, although low water absorption is a beneficial factor. Underfired bricks suffer badly. With calcium silicate brickwork, the higher the strength the greater the frost resistance. In stonework, fissures provide an easy passage for water to collect and freeze. Stonework which is laid with its natural bedding plane vertical is also susceptible to repeated splitting off of the face. Stones with low saturation coefficients (defined as absorption divided by porosity) are at least risk, especially if the pores which are open to water are coarse. Frost damage is only one of the causes of stonework decay. A number of other physical and chemical agents play a part, separately and in combination.

Sandstone is vulnerable to acidic rainwater, especially calcareous sandstones whose calcium carbonate cementing material within the stone is readily dissolved, thereby destroying the cohesion between sand grains. Limestone is essentially calcium carbonate and also suffers solution by acidic rainwater but in its case the action does not lead to a breakdown of the structure of the stone;

the weakening is a more gradual and more easily observed process. Where limestone and sandstone are used together, the action of acid on calcium carbonate can cause a rapid acceleration of the sandstone's decay.

Blockage of surface pores by dirt and redeposited salts can lead to the face of the stonework blistering and peeling off. This causes rapid erosion in areas blighted by pollution. The effect of sulphur gases is particularly serious, especially on limestones.

Crystallization just behind the stone face, caused by salts left behind during evaporation, has a similar effect. In this case it can be coastal areas, with salt-laden atmospheres, which suffer the most, and the worst damage sometimes occurs on the inside face, to which the salt is driven by evaporation.

Moisture and thermal stresses, particularly the former, can cause small-scale surface cracking in stonework, which can accelerate the other processes of decay. Tensile stress from any cause has this effect. There are few areas of permanent tensile stress in masonry. Stone lintels and walls which are eccentrically loaded or have developed leans or bulges provide occasional examples.

Stonework decay is more of a cosmetic than a structural problem, but in time it can create overstress, leading to bulging or cracking. Often this occurs in locally severe patches which are not difficult to repair.

Structural delamination

Often the integrity between internal and external skin is weak, especially if snap headers were used in construction (Figure 5.3). Where this has occurred, resistance to bowing is poor. Sometimes the skins separate.

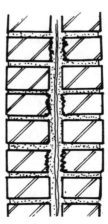

Figure 5.3   *Wall delamination*

A combination of: badly tied leaves, the inner one being of poor quality; no bond at cross walls; and poor restraint at floor levels introduces unexpected slenderness, which means that the wall's capacity to transfer permanent and temporary loads is only a fraction of what it should be. This may not be obvious by visual inspection. Gaps between external walls and floors may have been disguised by fillets (Figure 5.4), and redecoration may be hiding the growing separation between external walls and cross walls.

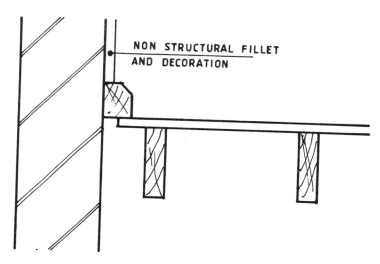

Figure 5.4 *Disguised lack of restraint*

Metal wall ties

Wall tie corrosion is very common and hard to detect, but rarely causes serious structural problems. In cavity walls built before 1982, the wall ties have a shorter life expectancy than the building. Rust occupies three times the volume of the parent steel, and rusting ties may cause horizontal thickening and splitting of bed courses at regular intervals. The more exposed parts of the building can be expected to show first.

But wall tie failure is not always visible, neither is it invariably spotted by boroscope inspection because corrosion may be rampant in the external leaf before being active in the cavity. As with timber decay, only systematic inspection, including the removal of some external bricks, is guaranteed to discover the problem.

Corrosion takes 13 to 75 years, depending on the type of tie used, type of mortar, quality of workmanship and the local environment. It is hastened by severe exposure, especially near the sea, by air pollution, sulphates in brickwork, poor quality ties, especially poor galvanizing, by lean mortar, and by aggressive constituents in the mortar such as black ash.

If a systematic inspection cannot be carried out, an assessment can be made of the likelihood of corrosion and the strength of the weakened wall. But, in the absence of evidence, pessimism has to rule any assessment. That usually means assuming the ties to have fully corroded, leaving the two leaves separate. When calculating the risk of the outer leaf failing under wind pressure, values must be chosen for flexural strength along bed joints and perpendicular to bed joints. One of the influences on flexural strength is the moisture content of the bricks when laid, so the calculation is going to be far from precise. Values must also be chosen for local wind force, panel size and degree of edge restraint. Unfortunately, regarding panel size and restraint, calculation would normally have to assume no assistance from cross walls and internal floors, because these elements only restrain the inner skin.

Panels with good restraint, especially at roof level where contact with rafters would guarantee precompression during flexure, have an excellent chance of survival without ties. Tall buildings, especially where there is no restraint for the external skin at floor levels, are at greatest risk. In practice, rusting is common but failures are rare.

Steel lintels were not generally galvanized until 1983 and some problems due to rusting of their webs and external ledges are to be expected.

Some of the early cavity walls, late nineteenth and early twentieth century, were tied by special masonry units which were usually formed with a slope across the cavity. These obviously do not decay but they can be ruptured by small differential movement between the two leaves, such as may be caused by consolidation or expansion.

Sulphate attack

Bricks which have a high sulphate content may initiate attack on the mortar. Such bricks are still being built into external walls. The sulphates are dissolved by rainwater and transported to mortar joints where they react with Ordinary Portland Cement in the mortar, causing it to weaken and expand. It is the expansion which usually causes most damage. If the external skin is restrained it may bulge outwards. It may, alternatively or in addition, lift the inner skin with it and the latter may then develop horizontal cracking, typically near roof level where its dead load is lightest. Lateral expansion is usually less evident but may be sufficient to cause slippage along the damp-proof course.

The mortar itself eventually whitens, cracks horizontally at mid-joint and spalls, but this may not be evident until the attack is advanced. When it is advanced, the mortar rapidly deteriorates and weathers.

Chimneys are prone to sulphate attack, because they are the most exposed parts of the building. Expansion is greatest where driving rain is greatest, and the chimneys therefore develop a leeward lean like trees near the coast.

Chimneys with no linings or with damaged linings can be weakened internally by the condensation of flue gases, which contain sulphur. A stack containing a number of flues can suffer from deterioration of the dividing walls (probably assisted by thermal stresses), resulting in a secret increase in the chimney's slenderness.

If external walls are rendered, the render will suffer damage as a result of sulphate expansion. It will develop cracks in line with brickwork joints or, if its bond to the brickwork is not good, larger cracks at wider centres, with pieces of render detaching themselves and falling.

Sulphate attack requires long periods of saturation. It is not usually serious on walls which are sheltered, or on walls containing strong mortar or sulphate-resisting mortar. Sulphates in the soil and groundwater can cause damage at foundation level, but serious cases are not common.

Chapter 6

CAUSES OF DAMAGE: GROUND MOVEMENT

The purpose of this chapter is to outline the common causes of structural damage which arise from movements of the ground.

Soil behaviour

The behaviour of soil is dominated by its particle size, its moisture content and its plasticity. Each separate cause of damage is influenced by at least two of those factors.

Recognition is based on particle size, or grading. Table 6.1 gives an idea of the limits of grading. More specific and comprehensive information is given by the British Standards on soil investigation and foundations, and by orthodox text books on soil mechanics. Mixtures of soils are more difficult to identify than single types such as sand, and their behaviour is more difficult to predict, although as a general rule the finer particles have a disproportionate influence. For example, a soil which is half clay and half sand will in essence behave as a slightly modified clay. Soils which contain at least 35 per cent silt and clay are called 'fine soils'; soils with less than 35 per cent silt and clay are called 'coarse soils'.

Settlement

Settlement under load occurs in all soils. It goes through three stages: an

Table 6.1   *Particle size recognition*

NAME	PARTICLE SIZE RANGE mm	SUB DIVISIONS mm	RECOGNITION
BOULDERS	200 +	–	VISUALLY UNMISTAKABLE
COBBLES	60 to 200	–	
GRAVELS	2 to 60	COARSE 20 to 60	60mm dia. UPPER LIMIT OF COARSE GRAVEL
		MEDIUM 6 to 20	20mm dia. VISUALLY UNMISTAKABLE / 6mm dia.
		FINE 2 to 6	2 ○ LOWER LIMIT OF FINE GRAVEL / UPPER LIMIT OF COARSE SAND
SANDS	0.06 to 2	COARSE 0.6 to 2	0.6 ● FEELS GRITTY, PARTICLES ARE VISIBLE AND RANGE IN SIZE ROUGHLY FROM GROUND PEPPER TO GRANULATED SUGAR. UNLESS IT IS MIXED WITH CLAY, IT CANNOT BE MOULDED AND UNLESS IT IS WET IT DUSTS OFF EASILY AFTER HANDLING.
		MEDIUM 0.2 to 0.6	0.2 .
		FINE 0.06 to 0.2	0.06
SILTS	0.002 to 0.06	COARSE .02 TO .06	FEELS SILKY, PARTICLES INVISIBLE OR BARELY VISIBLE. UNLESS IT IS MIXED WITH CLAY IT POWDERS WHEN REPEATEDLY ROLLED BETWEEN THE PALMS BUT DOES NOT DUST OFF EASILY. IN WATER IT DISINTEGRATES.
		MEDIUM .006 TO .02	
		FINE .002 TO .006	
CLAYS	LESS THAN 0.002	–	IF WET IT FEELS STICKY AND CAN BE MOULDED. REPEATED ROLLING BETWEEN THE PALMS PRODUCES THREADS WHICH MAY BE BRITTLE (IF NON–PLASTIC) OR MALLEABLE (IF PLASTIC). A BALL OF CLAY WILL EVENTUALLY TAKE A POLISH. DESICCATED CLAY CAN BE BROKEN INTO LUMPS WITH DIFFICULTY, BUT IS TOO HARD TO ROLL.

VISIBLE / INVISIBLE

immediate reaction, followed by consolidation, followed in some cases by a small and declining movement. Figure 6.1 shows the basic pattern. Well defined soils have their individual variations (Figure 6.2).

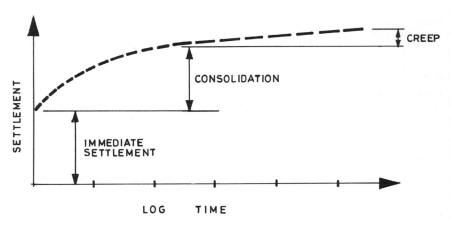

Figure 6.1   *Typical settlement curve*

On coarse soil the full settlement occurs almost immediately (Figure 6.2, curve a). On clay (Figure 6.2, curve b), settlement is largely the result of pore water being expelled by the load until equilibrium is reached, and the process takes longer because its rate is governed by soil permeability, which in clay is very low. Nevertheless, initial settlement is usually complete within a few years at most. In natural inorganic soil, creep is normally insignificant.

Peat settlement is caused partly by pore water expulsion and partly by compression of the soil skeleton itself. Immediate settlement and consolidation are both rapid. They are followed by creep, which is roughly proportional to log time – in other words the period between the first and tenth year would see as much settlement as the period between the tenth and hundreth (Figure 6.2, curve c). Peat consolidation can be regenerated by drainage (Figure 6.2, curve f).

Made ground consolidates under its own weight, and this will be partly or wholly complete before the building is constructed. The type of consolidation will depend upon its constituents and whether it was tipped or compacted. Most purely granular fills consolidate by between 1 per cent of their thickness (if well compacted) and 5 per cent (if tipped), and the process is largely complete within a year or so. Uncompacted clay may take five years or more to consolidate by 10 per cent. Mixed refuse takes much longer and its rate may vary if chemical reaction and gas production are involved. Unless it has been well compacted or subsequently improved, made ground has a definite creep stage.

Uncompacted made ground will still be loose, even if it has finished its consolidation and is well into its creep stage, so that when the building is constructed, settlement will usually be large. The pattern of settlement will be dominated, like the previous self-weight consolidation, by the ground's ingredients. Granular material will settle quickly; clay may take some time. There will also be an element of creep. Figure 6.2 shows imaginary curves for inert granular made ground (curve d) and mixed ground containing some degradable material (curve e).

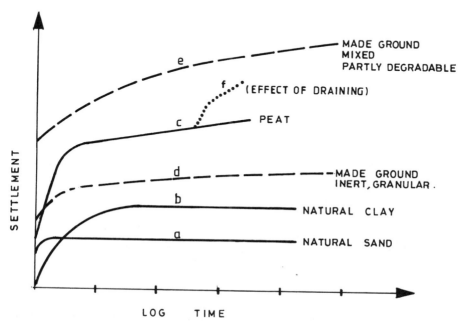

Figure 6.2   *Settlement for different soils*

Creep, whether of peat or made ground, is not usually a serious problem to buildings, unless there are large variations beneath the building of soil types or properties or thickness, but it may cause occasional cosmetic damage. In most cases, therefore, established buildings have virtually completed their settlement, even if they are on poor ground. Soil which is soft or loose will settle further if loads are redistributed by alterations, and this may need estimating, and possibly reducing, by design.

Foundation movement: shrinkable clay

Clay is classified by plasticity. This is defined by its liquid limit, plastic limit and plasticity index, the last term being the difference between the first two. These limits define the moisture content at which behaviour of the clay changes. They are in themselves arbitrary and unimportant, but they serve as a useful guide to engineering properties (Figure 6.3). For example, they are an approximate guide to shrinkability: the higher the plasticity value, the more shrinkable the clay.

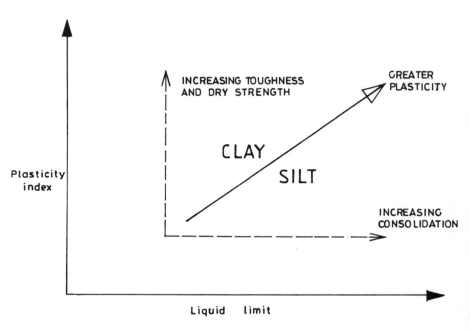

Figure 6.3   *Effect of plasticity*

Another factor which has an influence on shrinkability is the fraction of non-clay particles within the soil, such as sand and gravel. These modify shrinkability. When the clay fraction is above 35 per cent, clay is the dominating ingredient. There is no established point below which clay content is too low to affect shrinkage, but its influence appears to decline fairly rapidly below 30 per cent. (Clay content is rarely above 60 per cent in the UK.)

Within the UK, highly shrinkable clay is confined to the region southeast of a line drawn from the Humber, where the Trent joins it, to Exmouth on the south coast. Clays with some degree of shrinkability, however, are found in most other areas.

Shrinkable clay changes volume when its moisture content changes. As it dries out it shrinks, and it swells when it takes in moisture. Seasonal shrinkage and swelling occur within 1–1.5m of ground level. Foundations in this zone experience shrinkage as loss of support (subsidence) and swelling as a strong upward pressure (heave). They go through regular cycles of up and down movement, worse in some years than others, and occasional cosmetic damage is the result.

Trees considerably extend the zone of seasonal movement. As they grow, their root systems extend during the summer months and are capable of extracting moisture at a distance of 750mm from their hairy root ends. During winter, moisture returns to the soil. With a young tree, summer drying is matched by winter wetting, subject to weather fluctuations. A maturing tree may create a zone of permanent desiccation, or persistent deficit (Figure 6.4) within its root zone, which is never replenished until it dies and a long slow return to normal begins.

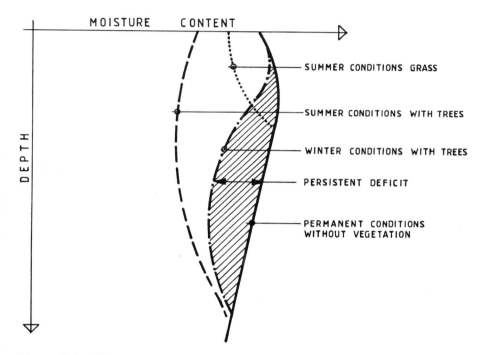

Figure 6.4   *Clay moisture profiles*

The National House Building Council's Practice Note 3 gives advice on clay and trees, and takes account of four main factors: soil plasticity, tree type, distance between tree and foundations, and geographical location. It divides soil plasticity into three categories: low, medium and high (Figure 6.5). Trees are either broad leaf or coniferous and are of low, moderate or high water demand. Simple charts combine these factors to give a safe relationship between distance from tree and depth of foundations. There is a slight reduction in required depths for locations north and west of London.

Practice Note 3 is design advice, of course. The average tree has a less extensive root system, but the occasional tree, more. No individual tree is predictable and no design guide can encompass all possible variations in site conditions. As a rule, on sites which are dry, for topographical or other

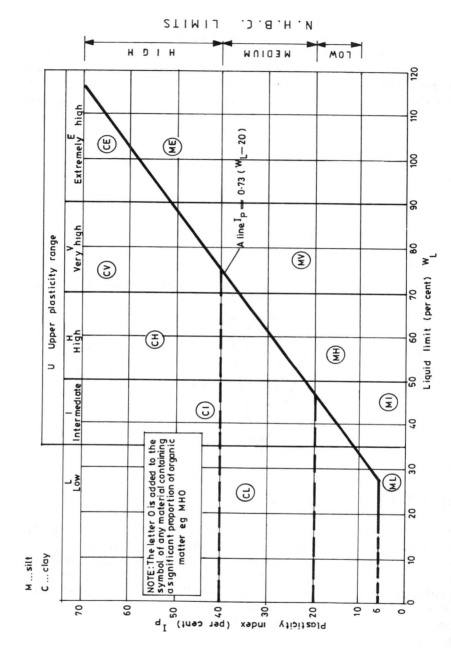

Figure 6.5 *Plasticity and shrinkability*

56

reasons, tree roots go deeper than average, and they spread wider on sites which are wet. They may be diverted by obstructions, and are capable of skirting root barriers or of course penetrating them if they crack.

Summits tend to be dry, especially if they have a capping of sand and gravel. On sites where dry granular material overlies clay, tree roots can be expected to go deeper than if clay were the only sub-soil. On the other hand, silt and granular material with a high water table may encourage shallow rooting. Valleys tend to be wetter than summits, especially close to river level. Sites are wet wherever they straddle a boundary between overlying permeable soil and underlying clay. Wherever natural drainage is interrupted by development there is a tendency for upstream areas to become wetter, although there may be an opposite tendency if the development diverts storm water into sealed drains.

When a tree is removed, the soil moisture content will increase. If the tree was previously causing only seasonal desiccation, it will normally return to equilibrium moisture content within one or two winters. If there has been a persistent deficit, the process is remarkably uncertain, and therefore unpredictable, for a number of reasons. First, the final moisture content, or equilibrium, is itself unpredictable. It depends on topographical and other factors. For the typical UK site it probably lies between 0.4–0.5 of the Liquid Limit, although some people link it to Plastic Limit (1.3 × Plastic Limit or Plastic Limit + 4 per cent being but two examples.

Second, progress towards equilibrium depends on the weather. Rainfall is so low in most shrinkable clay areas that, except for occasional short periods, precipitation is equalled by evaporation and transpiration, so that recovery of a deep desiccated zone is intermittent. It is quite possible, during prolonged dry periods, for monitoring to find no significant movement, giving the misleading impression that there is no more to come.

There are means of predicting the maximum likely heave, based on measured and predicted pore pressure, or on swelling tests. No single method is guaranteed to be accurate, and the best we can hope for is a reasonable idea of likely severity. Chapter 12 discusses this in a little more detail.

If a tree is causing subsidence to a building older than itself, tree removal is usually the most satisfactory solution. This ought to be done at the earliest sign of subsidence, otherwise the recovery period may be prolonged, owing to the formation of a persistent deficit, and that would condemn the building to a period of recurrent damage. If the damaged building is younger than the tree and if a persistent deficit has been established, there is no easy option. Further root growth (which may occur during a dry period even with a mature tree) might cause further subsidence, whereas removal of the tree, or its death, would almost certainly cause heave. The only safe technical solution would be to underpin to a stable level, removing all contact between building and desiccated clay.

Most cases of heave occur with new buildings, as a result of tree removal before construction. Areas previously used as ovens or kilns would have similar heave potential but are obviously very much less common. Moisture contents on any redeveloped land are likely to have strayed from equilibrium, although not usually by enough to create problems with foundations taken into undisturbed ground 1m or more below the surface.

Heave damage usually appears within five years of the incident which provoked it (usually tree removal). It accelerates to a peak, with declining activity after about ten years, but a run of dry years can delay onset, or cause a temporary pause. It is not uncommon to come across heave more than fifteen years after onset, but the rate has nearly always declined, by then, to the point where damage is only cosmetic. (Cases of slight heave would have a shorter run than fifteen years, of course. Very slight heave would be unnoticed.) During early active periods, damage can be severe. The movement cannot be arrested. It can only be avoided by separating the original foundations and ground floor from all contact with the heaving zone, transferring the building loads to a deeper, stable stratum.

Heave can operate laterally (Figure 6.6). The lateral pressure usually develops on the inside face of external foundations and would normally be fully resisted by the passive pressure of the external soil. But a small amount of external movement (which might arise, for example, from external shrinkage) would remove this resistance and allow full expression of the heave. Lateral heave can operate on the outside face, pushing foundations inwards. This is far less common simply because moisture content is more commonly higher beneath a building than outside, and because passive pressure is less often overcome on the inside face of foundations. When in full spate and unresisted, lateral heave can cause sudden and severe damage, because it acts against the wall's weakest plane.

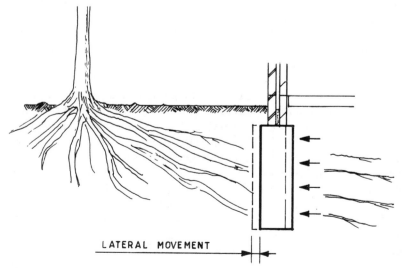

LATERAL   MOVEMENT

Figure 6.6   *Lateral heave*

Lastly, if heave is powerful enough to shift foundations it will usually shift a ground-supported floor slab. Clay subsidence, on the other hand, does not affect the ground floor slab at all unless the tree roots have penetrated beyond the external foundations. In the latter case, old buildings with shallow foundations are at greater risk than modern buildings whose foundations are usually a metre or more deep and offer more of a discouragement to lateral root spread.

Before 1980, foundations rarely included anti-heave precautions. This was the case even with engineer designed foundations such as pile and beam (and underpinning). All buildings older than 1980 but younger than a nearby tree are at risk of damage if the tree dies. The risk will vary with the circumstances but can be tested by carrying our moisture content profiles, described in Chapter 12, and of course by inspecting the foundations.

Subsidence on granular soil

Granular soil is stable unless subjected to vibration or acted upon by water. It may pack down or densify when vibrated and the two most common sources of vibration are traffic and pile driving, as discussed in Chapter 3. There is a rare and shortlived problem which can arise when vibrations affect ground before building. Such vibration may create differential density in the soil so that normal settlement under load is highest at the furthest point from the source of vibration.

Running water removes small granular particles, namely silt and fine sand, reducing the density of the remaining soil and thereby causing subsidence.

The most common cause of subsidence on natural silt and sand or sandy gravel is leaking drains. Broken water mains are less common, but when they do leak they produce the same effect quicker.

Sometimes soakaways are sited too close to a building. A distance of 5m is ideal but 3m is nearly always sufficient. Occasionally, rainwater downpipes simply discharge into or onto the ground, causing continual subsidence. More often, a fracture is found in the rainwater downpipe shoe connection to the stormwater drain, or in a foul drain leading from a gully or soil and vent pipe.

Where decayed old drains run alongside a building, large areas of footings might be disturbed by their leakage. More often, it is a local affair. Probing can establish its extent, in area and in depth. Figure 6.7 shows how a comparison can be made between disturbed and undisturbed areas using simple instruments, the simplest of all being a steel bar hammered into the ground to judge its resistance. More accurate tools are available, and this type of testing is discussed in Chapter 12.

Effect of water on clay

Subsidence due to leaching hardly ever affects clay soil, even though there is always a silt content, because the very low permeability prevents the water from penetrating except by slow seepage.

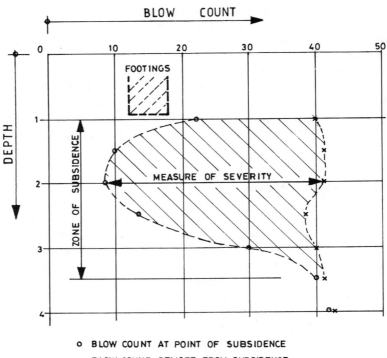

Figure 6.7   *Probing for subsidence*

In theory, water could cause subsidence in clay by softening. This is not unknown, but again low permeability usually comes to the rescue. Serious cases are confined to shallow foundations in organic or alluvial clays, clay which is already very highly stressed by heavy building loads, and soil where the clay content is low (signifying greater than average permeability and therefore deeper penetration by water).

Water from leakage can also cause heave of shrinkable clay. Once again, however, the soil's low permeability is its first line of defence. Water from a leaking drain, for example, will flow through the backfill round the pipe in preference to seeping into the clay, so the soil moisture content is in most cases increased only very close to the leak itself.

Subsidence on made ground

Beneath an established building, made ground will normally be stable, subject to any small creep movement. However, unless it was compacted when placed, or otherwise improved before building, it will not have the margin of safety over bearing pressure which is enjoyed by most natural soils. And it will be particularly sensitive to water leakage.

Inundation can also cause made ground to subside. This could occur by large fluctuations of the ground water level or by the occasional stormwater flood. Granular material consolidates under inundation by typically 2 per cent of its thickness; open cast backfill by 5 per cent; redeposited clay by 6 per cent. These figures are likely maxima, but are only rough. In rare cases, inundation has caused natural silt and sand to subside.

Subsidence on peat

Peat is best known for its weakness under load, but it is also highly plastic and, like shrinkable clay, it shrinks markedly when water is removed.

A building which has reached equilibrium above a peat layer may become damaged if tree roots dry out the peat and cause subsidence. Pumping can have a similar effect, and the effect can be rapid because peat is usually permeable unless it has at least a modest clay content, and it drains easily. Worse is to follow. The peat may start to decay if removal of water allows oxygen to it for the first time, and this leads to further collapse of the soil skeleton, with resultant subsidence. Curve f on Figure 6.2 shows the sort of regenerated movement which might arise from land drainage, or even short term pumping.

Subsidence on chalk

Chalk can subside when it is either weakened or dissolved by water, and the commonest problem is local solution by badly sited soakaways, broken drains or fractured water mains.

Chalk solution can take place below ground level and out of sight. The danger from that is usually undetectable before collapse. It is most likely to happen in areas where the chalk is overlain by a thin permeable sediment such as sand. As the solution pipe or cave slowly enlarges it reaches a size where the material above it can no longer sustain itself by arching across the hole, and it collapses (Figure 6.8). Collapse often happens after very heavy rain.

A similar type of failure can occur if water finds its way into old chalk workings which had previously been marginally stable. Chalk workings were normally sited in dry areas, above ground water level, and the source of the water which causes latter-day collapse is likely to be from leaking mains or drains rather than natural water courses.

In some cases, solution is not the problem; the chalk simply weakens catastrophically. This occurs most often with the upper chalk stratum which has been weathered and weakened since its deposition by many freeze/thaw cycles. Although strong enough to support most traditional buildings without undue settlement it can be quickly destroyed by an unexpected influx of water.

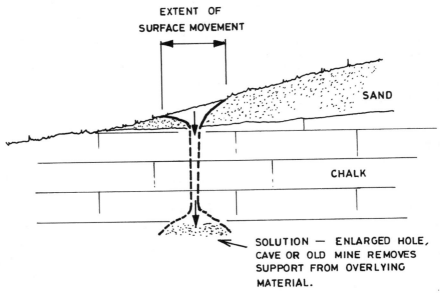

Figure 6.8 *Subsidence over chalk*

Weakening of chalk need not be the result of natural agents. Excavations which are left open, especially during winter, will encourage even strong chalk to break down and become putty. Heavy plant moving across the surface can, by liberating pore water from the chalk, also destroy its sensitive structure and encourage subsidence. Any building relying on the weakened chalk for support would be at greater than normal risk of settlement or, later and without warning, subsidence. Subsidence on chalk, then, can be local or widespread, mild or devastating, and the ground investigation should be carried out by a geotechnical engineer.

Chalk is also frost susceptible. Footings within 500mm of ground level are therefore vulnerable to heave, and projecting porches or small extensions are most vulnerable of all. In practice, few occupied buildings have suffered serious frost heave damage.

Limestone is also prone to solution, weakening and heave. Incidents are less common, although no less disastrous, because it is a stronger and more consistent material than chalk.

Landslip

Soil fails if it is made to stand too steeply with inadequate support. It can be a local problem when, for example, a brick retaining wall fails and a wedge of soil pushes forwards, or it can be more serious, involving mass movement.

Retaining wall failure can cause severe damage if the wall is part of the building (Figure 6.9). Failure is usually caused by unexpected loading or water building up behind the wall, adding its pressure to that of the earth.

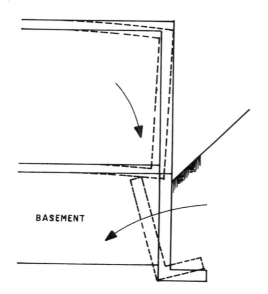

BASEMENT

Figure 6.9 *Retaining wall failure*

The less common but potentially more disastrous problem is mass movement, or slope instability. Slope instability beneath or uphill of a building is irresistible except by expensive civil engineering works. Movement may take the form of fairly shallow translational slides or rotational slips (Figure 6.10). Coarse soils are prone to shallow failure only. Fine soils may suffer shallow or rotational failure.

Granular soils such as sand and gravel are stable at slopes below their angle of friction, provided the ground is not weakend by seepage. Ground which contains clay, whether pure clay or clay-bound soil or clay strata within granular soil, is nothing like as predictable. This is because it is far more sensitive to changes in ground water or soil moisture content. A clay-dominated slope will undergo a very slow change in moisture content starting from the incident which last shaped it, which could be a previous slippage, a man-made cutting or wave action if it is a cliff. As a crude generalization, the moisture content rises near the face of the slope. This weakens the clay. So there is a very slow reduction in the factor of safety which corresponds with the change in moisture content. Equilibrium, and therefore minimum factor of safety, might take up to a hundred years to achieve. Meanwhile, further changes to the land gradient or ground water regime would, however slight, cause some deviation from the steady march to equilibrium. In fact it would set a new equilibrium. As long as the predicted end condition is favourable, in other words the clay will always have the strength to remain stable, the slope can be regarded as safe.

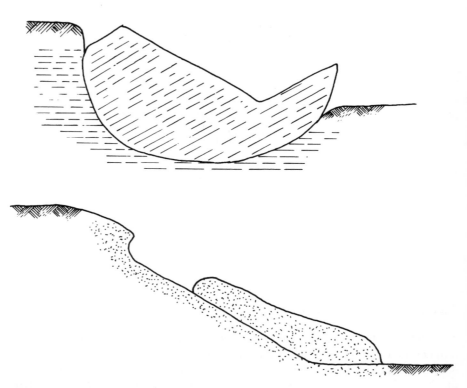

Figure 6.10   *Slope instability*

In theory, a factor of safety of 1 would be adequate, if the worst likely conditions were considered, but nothing in nature is exact. Analysis of failed slopes has yielded theoretical factors of safety above and below 1 (typically in the range 0.95–1.05). Slope stability analysis cannot be applied without specialist judgement. (Events which can affect slope stability are discussed in Chapter 17.)

Mining subsidence

Shallow coal mines are liable to cause subsidence by void migration (Figure 6.11). As the roof above the old mine workings disintegrates through lack of support, it forms a dome which in turn weakens and collapses. In this way, the void migrates upwards. It stops when either the collapsed material (which is bound to bulk in volume to some extent as it falls) clogs up the void, or a stable dome of rock forms, or the void breaks through to ground level. The last possibility is very likely to occur if the cover of rock above the worked seam is less than three times the thickness of the seam. A cover of five times the thickness is vulnerable; ten times is a low risk.

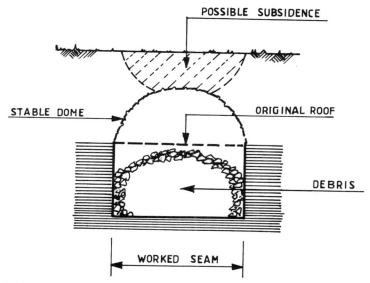

Figure 6.11 *Void migration*

Subsidence can also be caused by the failure of pillars or props left behind to support the roof. Such a failure may be due to a buckling or crushing of the pillars themselves, leading to progressive collapse, or to their punching into the roof or floor.

Shafts and entrances to underground mines (coal, tin, limestone or whatever) were often inadequately capped, sometimes merely blocked with, for example, timber, and afterwards given a light cover of fill. If the capping rots or dislodges, sudden collapse can occur. Any fill above the shaft will then spill into it, leaving a large subsidence crater (Figure 6.12). Sometimes old shafts have never been capped but have accidently filled with loose spillage over the years, in which case collapse can occur in the same way as with chalk swallow holes and workings (Figure 6.8).

Longwall mining causes a subsidence wave whose characteristics are well established. The building experiences this partly as a direct loss of support but often more damagingly as a tensile force at foundation level followed, as the wave passes, by a compressive force. The ideal foundations, in the absence of other hazard, would be a shallow reinforced raft placed on a low-friction bearing to minimize the direct forces. It is the tension which causes most damage to unprotected buildings. Cracks form at foundation level and taper upwards. No action is possible, other than temporary relief or repair, until the subsidence is complete, when the building can be assessed and final repairs carried out. If the wave crosses a fault line, subsidence of any building within 15m of the fault can be devastating.

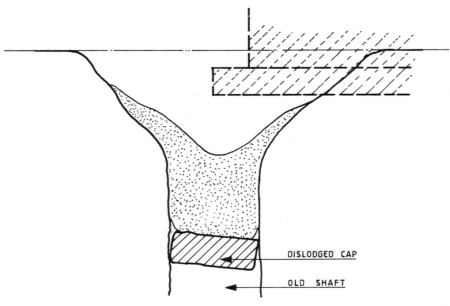

DISLODGED CAP

OLD   SHAFT

Figure 6.12   *Mine shaft subsidence*

Subsidence generated by longwall mining is generally complete twelve to eighteen months after the advancing face has passed.

Ground supported floors

At one time, ground floor settlement used to be the costliest major defect in new housing because little supervision was granted to the apparently simple process of site stripping, hardcore placing and concreting. Sometimes soft or organic soil was left after stripping, into which the hardcore sank over a period of time. More often, the hardcore itself was to blame. It was left loose, or contained degradable material, or else material (such as gravel rejects) which could not be properly compacted with standard site equipment.

Floor slab settlement usually appears early in the life of the building, but marginally stable hardcore may survive for many years before consolidating as a result of ground-water fluctuations or internal leakage.

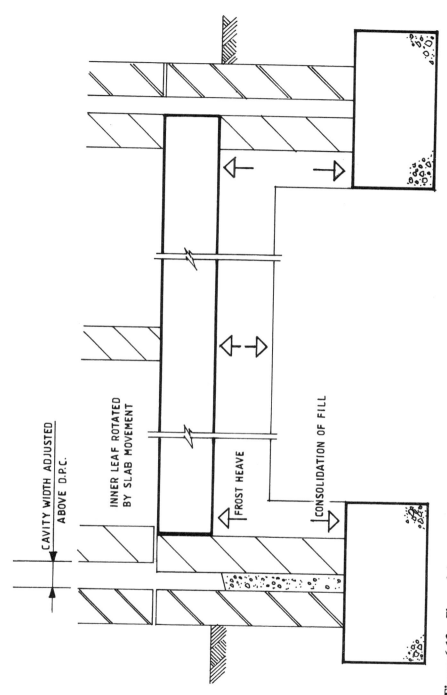

CAVITY WIDTH ADJUSTED
ABOVE D.P.C.

INNER LEAF ROTATED
BY SLAB MOVEMENT

FROST HEAVE

CONSOLIDATION OF FILL

Figure 6.13 *Floor slab movement*

There are now fewer instances thanks to a successful education campaign by the National House Building Council. The Council requires proper attention to constructing the ground floor, and a suspended ground floor must be used by their members whenever the depth of fill beneath it would exceed 600mm.

Symptoms of ground slab settlement are obvious but they can sometimes be confused with subsidence caused by tree root activity or the action of water. Upward movement of the ground slab can occur from clay heave. In fact, if the foundations are affected by heave, the slab nearly always is.

Another cause of upward movement is a high sulphate content in the hardcore. The use of unburnt colliery shale as hardcore once caused an epidemic of heave, but most of these cases have now been seen off. Water is needed for any form of sulphate attack. A high or fluctuating water table may saturate the hardcore across the full width of the building, and cause general uplift, but if the source of water is internal leakage or external run-off, damage will be concentrated in the wettest areas.

Upward movement of the ground slab can also occur from frost heave, either in the natural soil beneath it, if this is chalk or silt, or in the hardcore if this contains frost susceptible material. Ice lenses form, occupying 10 per cent more volume than water. Risk is greatest during building. Afterwards, soil temperature usually stabilizes above freezing point and ice formation is kept at bay, although an exposed perimeter might remain vulnerable.

Slab movement inevitably affects any walls built off it. This might include the internal leaf of external walls, whose connection to the slab may well be accidental (Figure 6.13).

Cracked, off-level or bumpy floor surfaces are often the fault of the screed alone, and not of the underlying slab. Many screeds contain too little cement inadequately mixed and poorly bonded to the slab, so that the finished product contains cement-rich nuggets within a lean matrix, sometimes with a thin rich surface forced by trowelling (occasionally this rich surface proves on closer examination to have been a rescue attempt using an additional, thin self-levelling screed). Screed thickness often varies between wide limits.

A screed with a selection of such faults will be more prone to crack due to shrinkage, or to indent or break up due to point loads or foot traffic, and this could give the misleading impression that the floor slab itself has failed.

Chapter 7

THE INFLUENCE OF FOUNDATIONS

Potential foundation problems cannot be understood without inspecting the foundations. They are not simply the contact face between building and ground. They influence the building's behaviour by their own strengths and weaknesses

Effect of stiffness

Only a building devoid of any stiffness would distort in total sympathy with ground movement; only an infinitely stiff building could impose a uniform displacement upon the ground. Real buildings respond according to the combined stiffness of their foundations and superstructure, or rather the ratio of that combined stiffness to the stiffness of the soil which supports them.

This is a well-established notion, which is illustrated in Figure 7.1. Diagram (a) is the infinitely flexible case; diagram (b) the infinitely stiff. Neither is real. Diagram (c) shows a building with a reasonable foundation and superstructure stiffness. Diagram (d) is the same building, but with the first floor supported on columns. The columns would tend to isolate the superstructure as far as its contribution was concerned, so that the stiffness of the building as a whole would derive mainly from its foundations. A low bond damp proof course would have a similar effect on a lightweight building.

The obvious difference between flexible and stiff buildings is that the former undergo greater differential settlement for the same average settlement. Diagrams (e) and (f) show this more specifically. Both are assumed to apply the same eccentric load to the soil, and this causes the same average settlement (or nearly so), but the stiffer building responds to the eccentricity by tilting rather than bending, and its differential settlement is likely to be less. Certainly its angular distortion, the main damager of superstructures, will be less.

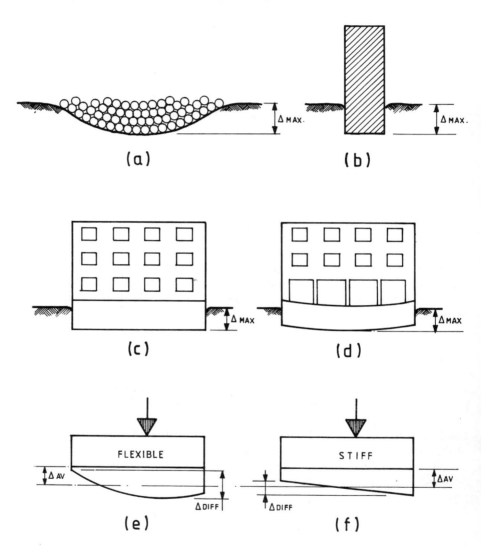

Figure 7.1   *Effect of stiffness on movement*

The transition from very high to very low differential settlement is not easily defined for traditional buildings. It might be achieved by a ten-fold increase in foundation thickness, if all other circumstances conspired, which is the difference between 150mm traditional strip and 1 500mm trench fill, but that is only a rough illustration. Nevertheless, even a qualitative knowledge of stiffness can play its part in judging the possible effect of ground movement.

Since it is the ratio of the building to soil stiffness which counts, buildings are more likely to settle uniformly or to tilt on soils with very low moduli, such as soft alluvium or peat, than on soils with high moduli such as stiff clay or dense sand.

Raft foundations are usually designed with careful attention to their bending strength, but sometimes their stiffness is neglected. A raft which is thin compared with its plan dimensions may be much stronger than traditional foundations but no stiffer. It would be capable of deforming considerably without actually failing. If it passes on such deformation to the building it supports, as it must, then it may inflict serious damage. Only a raft which (together with its superstructure) is stiff compared with the supporting soil will be able to smooth out the differential settlement sufficiently to avoid damage.

Stiff rafts are not immune from soil/structure stiffness problems. On soft variable ground, or with eccentric loading, they tilt. Small extensions are prone to tilting, which is acceptable up to a point, unless they are designed to match centre of load with centre of raft.

A high building-to-soil stiffness ratio reduces differential movement in all types of ground movement, including subsidence and heave, as well as settlement. Unfortunately, heaving soils are stiff.

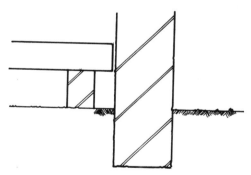

Figure 7.2 *Straight footings*

Changing styles

Foundation styles have changed over the years. Old brick buildings often have no foundations as such but were simply built off the ground (Figure 7.2) from a level deemed to be below the vegetable soil and any other superficial loose material. In heavier buildings, the bearing pressure was reduced by widening the wall below ground level. It is not uncommon to find a layer of hardcore, sometimes bound with lime mortar, immediately beneath the bottom course of brickwork (Figure 7.3). This will have created a deeper but probably no less flexible foundation. Brick foundations were sometimes arched along the line of the wall to strengthen them in weak ground (Figure 7.4), and heavy buildings, especially in difficult ground, were sometimes built off vertical timber piles.

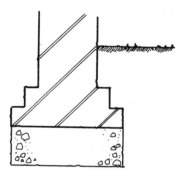

Figure 7.3   *Corbelled footings*

The studs of early timber frames were often inserted directly into post holes in the ground, but most surviving buildings have some sort of foundation, either in the form of a timber sole plate or a stone plinth. The sole plate was usually oak. In heavy buildings, individual columns were sometimes built off a nest of oak spreaders. In many buildings the original plate has been replaced by a brick or stone plinth. The manufacture of Portland Cement made concrete strip footings (Figure 7.5) the most popular type of foundation by the early twentieth century.

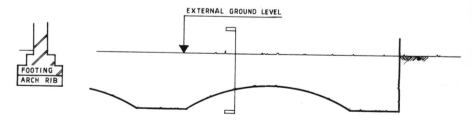

Figure 7.4   *Arch footings*

By the mid twentieth century foundations were getting deeper. Bricklaying inside a trench is awkward, and trench fill (Figure 7.6) became an attractive alternative. Cement manufacturers recommended it for speed of construction, and on the grounds that friction between concrete and trench sides would add to the foundation's load bearing capacity, although the latter proved to be true only until summer shrinkage destroyed contact.

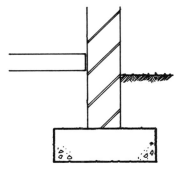

Figure 7.5   *Traditional strip footings*

Until the 1970s not many foundations were taken deeper than 900mm, but afterwards builders became more aware of problems such as made ground and trees in clay. Also, Local Authorities and the National House Building Council directed more of their inspecting resources towards foundations. This made trench fill even more popular. Some ridiculously deep and (in an attempt to reduce concrete quantity) narrow foundations were built in the late 1970s and early 1980s, before their disadvantages were realized.

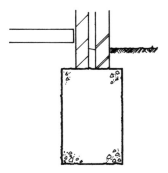

Figure 7.6   *Trench fill foundations*

Figure 7.7 shows how trench fill can get out of its depth. A very deep excavation (1) can, if the operator fails to keep the machine level, be installed out of vertical (2). If the excavation is narrow (3) and the trench slightly off line, the foundation loads will be seriously eccentric (4). Many are. Many survive, but there is a risk of rotation and damage if the poor construction is followed by unwelcome events such as internal pressure (5) not resisted externally (6). In 1989 the National House Building Council sounded a warning by requiring their members to employ engineers to design trench fill foundations for depths in excess of 2.5m.

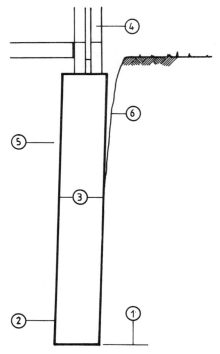

Figure 7.7   *Very deep trench fill*

Trench fill was sometimes nominally reinforced with, for example, two bars near the top and two near the bottom. The bars gave it strength to go with its stiffness. In the case of low-rise buildings, it transformed the foundation into a beam with greater bending capacity than the entire superstructure, enabling it to span safely large distances across soil of variable quality (but it was no answer to lateral pressure, unfortunately). Sometimes, trench fill behaviour can only be understood by finding out, using a powerful covermeter, whether reinforcement has been used. The standard of steelfixing was often unsophisticated and on rare occasions it introduced problems by creating weak points at discontinuities in the reinforcement. Differential movement would then concentrate at such discontinuities, magnifying what might otherwise have been cosmetic damage (Figure 7.8). Similar problems could occur at badly formed joints in plain concrete.

By the 1980s, builders were making greater use of piles and deep pads (Figure 7.9). At the same time, anti-heave precautions, for use in shrinkable clay, were improved and were being used more intelligently (Figure 7.10).

Raft foundations have been in use ever since Portland Cement became available. Early twentieth century rafts were flat and unreinforced. By the mid twentieth century, reinforcement was in general use and numerous shapes were in and out of fashion (Figure 7.11).

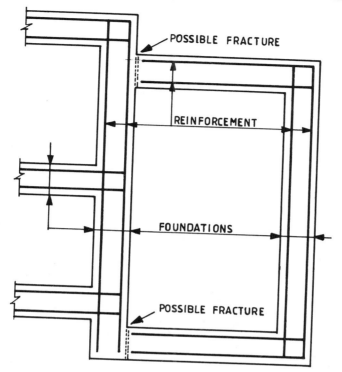

Figure 7.8 *Defect caused by poor steelfixing*

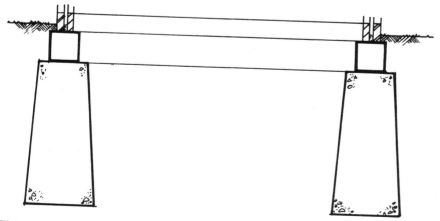

Figure 7.9 *Beam and pad foundation*

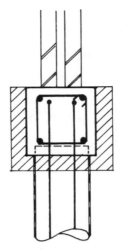

Figure 7.10   *Pile and beam foundations*

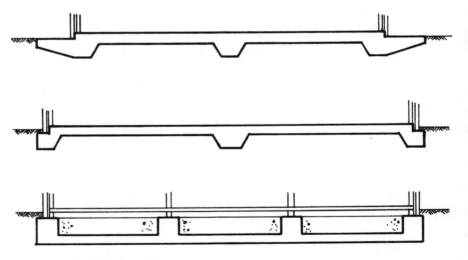

Figure 7.11   *Raft foundations*

Behaviour of foundations

The shallow brick footings, without benefit of concrete strip or trench fill, were most prone to large settlement, and remain prone to movement from additional loading or ground disturbance.

The same is true of timber sole plates. They have the additional disadvantage of decay. That is rarely catastrophic because even completely rotten timber will transfer loading as long as it is restrained within the surrounding soil, but it does of course leave the building vulnerable to even small alterations. A decayed plate will also infect studs connected to it.

In soft ground shallow foundations sometimes rotated as the soil yielded under load. Any such movement is most unlikely to be still active, but the evidence would serve as a warning against increasing the loading without making improvements.

Foundations in the top 500m which are in silt or fine sand or chalk are vulnerable to frost heave, although this does not often lead to damage in occupied buildings. All types of shallow footing can be damaged by excavations close to them (Figure 7.12). This is discussed in Chapter 17.

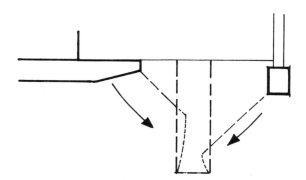

Figure 7.12 *Damage caused by excavation*

Settlement under load became less with the introduction of concrete footings. Trench fill, because of its stiffness, behaved even better, apart from its peculiar weaknesses which have already been discussed.

Beam and pad foundations have a good record. Some failures have occurred when pads were not made deep enough, most often in made ground and shrinkable clay, and usually because the ground problem was recognized but not fully understood. Pads were generally dug by mechanical excavator whose reach depended on the machine type, its condition and the skill of the operator, but was limited to typically 3m or so, and there is no doubt that in some cases the machine was simply unable to penetrate the hazard. The builder then faced the dilemma of abandoning the excavations or taking a risk at whatever depth could be managed. The latter course was often chosen, a decision which always appears cynical in hindsight, when its consequence has to be faced. However, on-site panic can introduce a desperate optimism into one's judgement of ground conditions. On small developments, especially, these crises are still handled by people inexperienced in soil mechanics, working in difficult conditions and perhaps anxious not to waste the concrete queueing at the entrance in ready-mix trucks.

Searching for tree roots in shrinkable clay is another activity which punishes false optimism, In theory, foundations on shrinkable clay sites from which trees have been removed will be safe if taken a reasonable distance below previous root activity (assuming allowance is made for lateral heave and friction on foundation sides). In practice, a designer's advice to excavate 'below all sign of tree roots' cannot be guaranteed on site. Failures have occurred even when excavation has been attended by experienced building inspectors and other professionals. Subsequent investigations, made with the usual benefit of hindsight, have then found other layers of roots deeper than the foundations, which were obviously invisible during construction.

There is no opportunity to detect deeper than expected root layers if judgement is based on trench inspection. Even if the site is peppered with deep inspection holes off the line of foundations, so as not to interfere with them, the risk of missing tree roots is only reduced and not eliminated.

Deep unshored excavations are difficult to clean out because they cannot be properly inspected from ground level. Unless they are cleaned, the concrete may be poured on top of debris which has fallen in from the sides. Misshapen pads and trench fill foundations are a sign of instability during excavation which might, if it led to debris collecting on the bottom, have created conditions for larger than normal settlement.

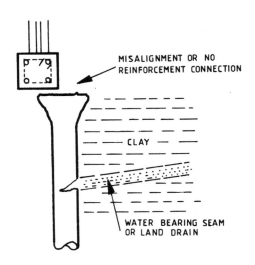

Figure 7.13   *Pile faults*

Short-bored piles were often, before the 1970s, too short (sometimes 2-3m). Those which have survived have proved themselves, but may not be capable of taking new loads, or of living with maturing trees, if the soil is shrinkable clay. Otherwise the success of piles has depended very much on workmanship. The two worst faults have been the failure to connect pile top to beam and the collapse of the pile shaft, either during or soon after boring (Figure 7.13). In both cases the pile is bad and simply cannot take its load, which is instead transferred to the soil beneath the ground beams. If this overloads the soil, there is a local failure of the foundations. (The soil may not of course be overloaded. It may hold firm until seasonal movement or some other agent removes support. As always, the detailed cause must be found if conclusions are to be credible.)

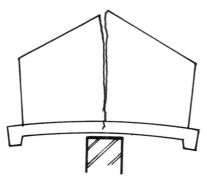

Figure 7.14 *Hard spot*

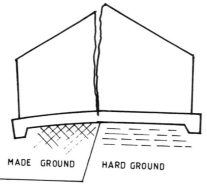

MADE GROUND HARD GROUND

Figure 7.15 *Variable ground*

Rafts have capacity to spread loads over areas of soft ground. They do not, unless they are unusually stiff, cope as well with hard spots (Figure 7.14) or extreme variations in ground conditions (Figure 7.15), as already mentioned.

The problems which are caused by steps in foundation depth are overstated. As long as all parts are beyond seasonal movement and foundation loads are relatively light, or alternatively are evened out by varying the foundation width, then no significant damage is likely to be caused by varying the depth, or even the type, of foundation. That is, of course, an observation on

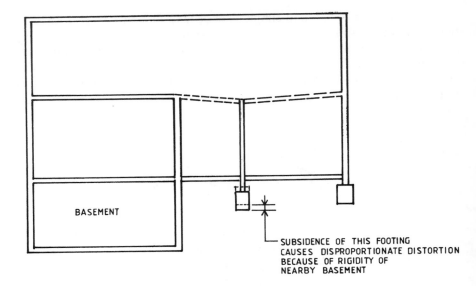

Figure 7.16   *Differential subsidence*

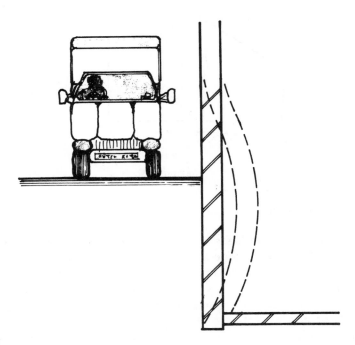

Figure 7.17   *Damage due to increased load*

established buildings rather than a design recommendation. Problems have occurred. Old buildings with basements have undergone very large differential settlements because the deep basement walls have been rigid, whereas the very shallow adjoining walls may have settled by several centimetres. Such movement should now be extinct, but the same building might be prone to a new incident such as subsidence (Figure 7.16).

Another problem with basement walls is that they are sometimes founded practically at basement floor level. This means that excavation in the basement may undermine them. It also suggests that they have, as retaining walls, precarious stability which might be damaged by some innocent change such as providing a paved area to allow vehicular access next to the building (Figure 7.17).

Chapter 8

DESK STUDY

Local knowledge, if it has the ring of truth rather than the thud of rumour, is a useful part of the investigator's stock of information. Desk studies complement it. It is worth keeping a library of general information, such as geological maps and memoirs, which can be applied quickly and easily to every job. Information which has to be collected or ordered adds to time and cost, so its potential value has to be questioned each time.

Drawings

Drawings of recent buildings may still be held by the Local Authority Building Control. Information that might assist the appraisal of older property is harder to find. In the case of prestigious buildings, architects or contractors who have carried out work may have some drawings, the owners may have past reports and drawings, and the Local Records Office may contain useful items such as accounts of old fire damage or substantial rebuilding.

Maps

First edition reprints of one-inch Ordnance Survey maps are inexpensive. They highlight ancient and modern excavations, valleys, water courses, settlements and woodland, as known during the 1800s. A more detailed search can be made by studying all available editions of the larger scale maps, which in many areas go back to 1850 or earlier and show excavations, land use and buildings at a useful scale. Earlier town centre maps are available in Records Offices.

Aerial photographs

Aerial photographs cover only comparatively recent times (post-World War II), but often reveal important features such as landslips, old pits, filled ponds and previous vegetation, as well as changes to the size and shape of buildings. Sub-surface features such as old dykes, swallow holes, buried pipelines and boundary lines can also show up vividly on an aerial photograph.

Infra-red photography, with sophisticated data processing, is capable of detecting foundation outlines and other sub-surface features to a high resolution, but it requires special commissioning which puts it beyond the resources of the run-of-the-mill investigation.

Geology and soil maps

Geological maps help to plan the ground investigation, by showing what to expect and therefore what foundation problems to expect. It is important to study the 'Drift' or 'Solid and Drift' maps. 'Solid' maps do not show the recent deposits which overlie the older rocks. Although mapping is imprecise, it is usually good enough to show the predominant sub-soil, which may be of a single type or may include a good deal of local variation. Features which influence foundation behaviour may be detected, such as boundaries between permeable and impermeable soil where the area may be waterlogged, or the presence of faults which might exaggerate mining subsidence.

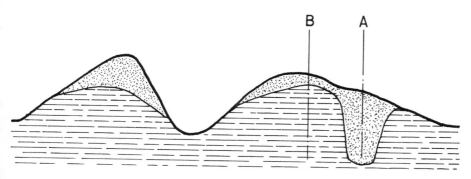

Figure 8.1 *Variable ground*

Figure 8.1 shows an ancient valley filled with sand and gravel during glaciation. Below the level of glaciation, the predominant soil was a shrinkable clay. A borehole at 'A' was used first to prepare a foundation design for a building at that position and then to prepare a foundation design for a building at 'B', roughly 60m away. The local geological map had a cross-section which highlighted the difference in thickness of the sand and gravel, and helped to explain why the foundations at 'B' had failed. The area was thickly wooded. Whereas this had little implication at 'A', it led to heave at 'B'. (The designer might have avoided failure by consulting the map originally).

Geological maps show landslips and made ground, but the information is incomplete, not least because the data were prepared a long time ago and have not yet been universally updated.

Another disadvantage is in the classification. The categories are based on age and can include soils of widely differing properties within a single stratum name. The Soil Survey of England and Wales is based on a more recent and systematic gathering of data, and does not suffer from the same disadvantage. It recognizes all variations in soil type. It also shows more clearly some of the important recent deposits such as alluvium, which may be soft and wet and possibly organic. Unfortunately, town centres are not covered. The other disadvantage of soil survey maps is that the exploration was superficial and reports only on the top metre of soil. In certain areas of Fenland, for example, there is peat 1.5–2m below ground level not revealed by the soil survey.

The disadvantages of geological and soil survey maps spring from the fact that they were simply not prepared for building investigators. Subject to these accidental limitations, they are invaluable and cheap. The discovery on site of a soil, or sequence of soils, which geological and soil data would not have predicted, is cause for suspicion. It suggests that the building may be on made ground.

Books on regional geology, and geological memoirs, are a useful supplement to maps. The more they are consulted the better they become.

The British Geological Survey's *Directory of Mines and Quarries* lists most of the commercial mines. The Health and Safety Executive may help with others. British Coal can advise on coal mines in general, and specifically on recent or expected subsidence and abandoned workings. The police can sometimes advise on pits dug for special purposes, such as the burial of diseased animals.

Between desk and site, clues may be available from adjacent properties and local features such as street names. The condition of other buildings may suggest whether there is a widespread problem. Names can suggest previous usage. Unnatural topography and sharp differences in age between buildings in the same vicinity suggest redevelopment, possibly on poor ground. These clues are only superficial but they can provide pointers, sometimes invaluable pointers.

Chapter 9

VISUAL INSPECTION

Every inspection should be planned. In the case of a large building requiring a comprehensive investigation before refurbishment, this would normally mean a special visit and a study of background information. In the case of a small building, the whole job has to be completed within hours, and the planning takes place in the first few minutes. It is no less important.

Planning should start as a rehearsal of the full inspection, noting the type and age of the building, its likely problems, and its evident problems. At the same time, special difficulties, such as access or uncertain structural layout, should be confronted while there is still time to sort them out. That preview then guides the routine inspection which follows. At that stage, judgement should be suspended. Even if the structual problems look straightforward, the visual inspection at least should be recorded in full with an unbiased mind.

Coverings

Coverings and decorations are a handicap, especially if no removal at all is permitted. They may be disguising unrepaired structural damage or they may be confusing the issue with their own structurally irrelevant damage.

Plasters and renders are sensitive and will generally betray structural movement, although its pattern will be less clear than if there were no covering, so it is safe to assume that any problem that has arisen since the covering was placed (or last repaired) will be evident. Ceramic tiles and paper decorations are also sensitive, but external hanging tiles disguise anything short of collapse.

Damage record

Damage should be recorded as accurately as possible using an infallible convention. In the case of brickwork (Figure 9.1), the exact position, pattern and width (including all variations of width) of every crack should be noted. Features such as lipping, vertical displacement and spalling are of particular interest.

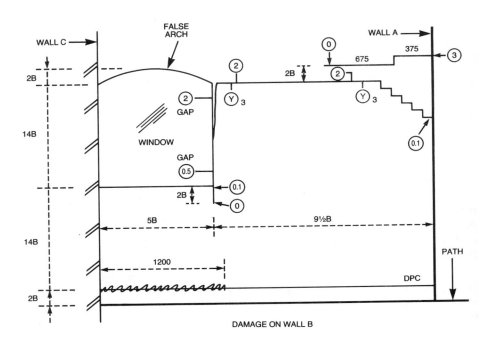

Dimensions are given in mm or brick modules, eg 2B = 150mm vertically and 450mm horizontally. Stepped cracking, unless dimensioned otherwise, is assumed to run 75mm vertically and 112.5mm horizontally, ie through beds and perps. Crack widths are given by figures in circles eg ② Lipped cracking is indicated by Ⓨ 3, the symbol appearing on the depressed side (furthest from observer) and the figure referring to the measure of lipping. ⌁⌁⌁⌁⌁⌁ indicates spalling.

Figure 9.1 *Recording damage on site*

Blockwork, stone or concrete, is a similar material. Damage rarely follows quite the same pattern that it would with brickwork, as often demonstrated by modern brick and block cavity walls. Low density blockwork cracks through the blocks in preference to perpends. In stonework, the crack line will depend on the thickness of mortar joints and degree of mortar adhesion. Nevertheless, the basic position, line and taper of cracking tells the same tale with all types of masonry.

Where the inner skin of an external wall is in modern timber frame, its pattern of damage usually consists of separation between panels, especially above openings. The panels themselves are almost damage proof. This difference in behaviour between timber frame and external skin may disrupt the ties between them.

Initial interpretation

When the record of visual inspection is complete, it is safe to make a tentative interpretation. This guides other parts of the investigation. Occasionally, it misguides, and is renounced when better evidence accumulates. Opinion must not harden too early. It helps to remember the obvious point that nearly all masonry damage is tensile and represents strain at right angles to the line of the crack.

In Chapter 3, the mechanism of drying shrinkage, temperature and moisture movement was discussed. Damage from any of these events is a reflection of frustrated horizontal movement. Vertical movement usually takes place freely, unless there is differential behaviour between the two skins arising from sulphate attack, consolidation or volume change. Figure 4.7 showed some likely symptoms.

Although the subject is traditional buildings, differential movement between steel or reinforced concrete frame and brickwork is worth a passing mention. With good detailing, frame and brick should coexist happily, but without good detailing serious damage can be imposed on the brickwork by the frame. Concrete frames shrink. The building as a whole will expand and contract, and whereas frames do so elastically and without harm to themselves they will shunt brickwork along and damage it unless joints are provided. Under load, frames also behave differently to masonry. In particular they may sway to an extent perfectly acceptable to themselves but not to any rigidly attached masonry.

Returning to traditional building: overstressing of masonry purely as a result of normal gravity loads is rare. When it does occur it is usually at beam or lintel bearings where the masonry may be split by the tension which forms immediately below a highly compressed zone. Other types of movement, not associated with gravity loads, also concentrate at bearings, and are more common. Overstressing is usually distinguished from these other causes by the position of the damage (Figure 3.11) and lack of horizontal movement.

Foundation movement can be tested by imagining the wall as a beam (Figure 9.2). The beam may tilt (Figure 9.2a), or it may deform in shear (Figure 9.2b) or in bending (Figure 9.2c). Actual behaviour may be a combination of all three, depending on a number of factors. (The beam analogy is discussed in more detail in Chapter 16.)

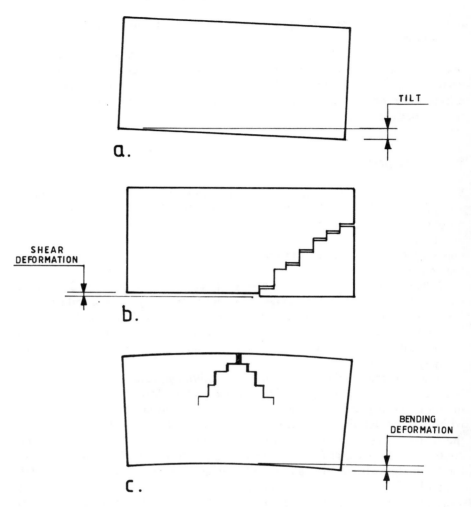

Figure 9.2 *Modes of deformation*

The greater the length-to-height ratio, the greater is the influence of bending and the more likely it is that damage will form as tensile bending strain. For solid walls, formulae derived from bending theory would predict crack behaviour fairly accurately. Three other factors have a strong influence:

- *Mode of deformation* When bending is the cause of cracking, it matters whether the deformation is sagging or hogging (Figure 9.3). In sagging mode, tension must develop at the bottom where there will be some resistance from the foundations. This resistance will be large if the foundations are deep reinforced trench fill, but minimal if they are shallow brick footings, although in the latter case there would still be some help from friction between earth and footings. Brick walls which have a felt or slate damp-proof course may find this horizontal layer to be the weak point. It is not at all uncommon to find that cracking immediately above the damp-proof course is a scale higher than below, the difference being accounted for by slippage along it. In hogging mode, there is little resistance to propagation at roof level. Hogging does more damage than the same amount of sagging.

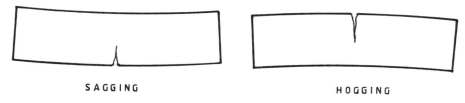

SAGGING   HOGGING

Figure 9.3   *Bending damage*

- *Influence of openings* Openings reduce both bending and shear resistance, especially the latter. Terraces whose front walls are heavily pierced are likely to fracture in shear at edges of openings. A single storey wall with a door in it almost becomes two separate walls with a weak link between them. Even on lightly pierced walls, damage is more often than not attracted to openings, because of their weakening effect. If the appearance of damage at an opening is a shift from the position where it might otherwise have formed, its cause might also be harder to understand from visual inspection alone and hence, in many cases, the need for a distortion survey and ground investigation.
- *Restraint* Restraint stiffens resistance to movement. At the same time, it transfers the effects of it to other parts of the building. Figure 9.4 shows an example where the tendency of the right hand wall to lean is resisted by the first floor and roof which in turn impart a horizontal force to the left hand wall, and the latter may respond by bending and cracking along a bed course. A long bed course crack is a typical sign of remote movement.

In well-built cellular construction, especially where room sizes and therefore wall-panel sizes are small, quite local movement can cause widespread hairline cracking at wall/ceiling and other junctions. Although cosmetically disappointing, it is a healthy sign. For example, an old and robust building underwent a subsidence which proved to be local and non-progressive. It suffered no significant loss of integrity because the slight movement was successfully restrained by walls and floors. But the lath and plaster ceilings had become brittle with age. They were also beginning to lose bond with the joists. Every millimetre of strain registered on the ceilings, causing widespread damage and giving the false impression that a more general problem had developed.

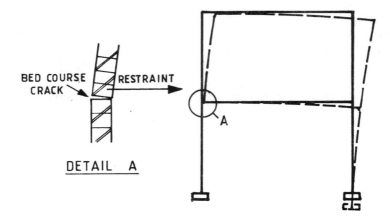

Figure 9.4   *Damage and restraint*

Timber frame

Mediaeval timber frame accepts gross distortions without damage. Visual inspection cannot be as direct as with brickwork, and nor can structural appraisal always be as confident. It is wise, at the planning stage of the investigation, to decide first what type of timber frame construction has been used. It may follow one of the standard patterns or it may be unorthodox; it may be unaltered, or (more likely) it may have suffered many alterations; its principal members may be on view, or they may now be rendered over.

The visual inspection itself can only seek clues towards movement. Racking (Figure 9.5) or rotation (Figure 9.6) are the most common responses to structural movement and may be detected through damage to finishes or joints. All accessible joints should be closely inspected. Not only may they advertise structural movement (Figure 9.7) but they may be the weakest points in the structure; not all joints have the capacity to withstand severe distortion and in some cases they may need urgent improvement. Joist to beam connections without horizontal restraint (Figure 9.8) are often found to have reached a delicate stage.

Deterioration

Structural appraisal needs to consider the extent of deterioration, or at least be able to rely on its absence. The detection of damp, rot, infestation and material decay therefore has an impact on many structural appraisals, which is considered in brief outline in the following notes.

The age and style of the building would suggest its degree of susceptibility. Modern buildings have few built-in timbers and have had relatively short

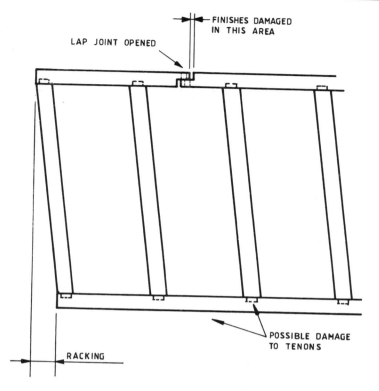

Figure 9.5 *Racking*

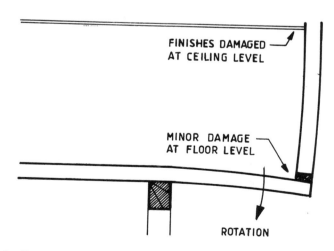

Figure 9.6 *Rotation*

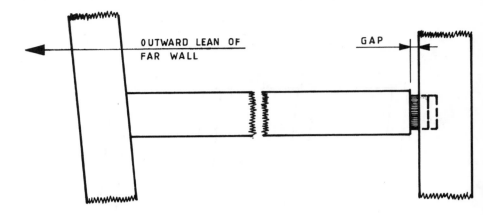

Figure 9.7 *Movement at joint*

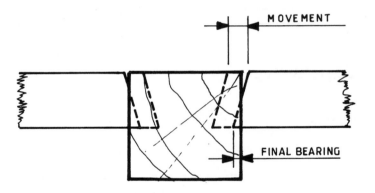

Figure 9.8 *Distorted connection*

exposure to attack. They are unlikely to be suffering from any significant form of deterioration, except possibly wall-tie failure, and are extremely unlikely to be on the verge of serious structural damage as a result of any deterioration. A risk as low as that often justifies no attention at all. Its lack must of course be acknowledged. Old neglected buildings are likely to have at least some local problems, not all of which will be obvious. Rainwater from a chronic roof leak can journey one or two floors down and do its damage there. An investigation of such a high-risk building should at least go to the next stage of inspection, if only to sound a warning.

The next stage of inspection is the recognition, mainly from external and remote viewpoints, of situations which might encourage damp and therefore timber deterioration – leaking rainwater goods and the like, as discussed in Chapter 5.

The following stage, if justified by the brief, would be a closer look, internally, for indicators of moist conditions and insect activity. The presence of mould on plaster, masonry or wood, or of harmless fungi, would suggest that conditions are ripe for rot, even if the process is not yet under way. Exit holes demonstrate infestation, which may or may not be active. Bore dust would suggest some recent activity. On the other hand the absence of exit holes and bore dust is not a guarantee that there is no infestation, since wood-boring insects spend nearly all their life below the surface, and if conditions which encourage rot are present anywhere, the probability of insect attack should also be admitted.

Moisture meters, which give readings based on electrical resistivity, will detect wet conditions and can be used as indicators. Readings are expressed, in percentage terms, as weight of moisture divided by weight of dry wood. Timber with readings below 20 per cent can be regarded as safe. Above 40 per cent, the conditions are approaching the ideal for rot and insect attack. Certain agents falsify the readings. These include some preservatives, fire retardants and stored materials, as well as temporary surface condensation. Fortunately, the reading errors are nearly always on the high side. They can be avoided by probing below the surface.

Advanced rot and infestation can sometimes be sounded by a hammer tap which produces a dull thud in decayed timber instead of the usual healthy ring. Drilling may find hollows and soft interiors. Only cores, intelligently positioned, can give any useful idea of the extent of the decay.

Serious decay may overshadow the structural problems. It would require a strategy for: immediate treatment, to control present deterioration; long-term improvement, to deter recurrence; and structural analysis, to determine the value of remaining timber. The strategy should be informed by a systematic inspection carried out by an experienced surveyor.

External masonry decay is apparent and requires no more than a careful examination, taking into account the strength reducing factors mentioned in Chapter 5. Internal decay can only be seen if the removal of coverings is allowed, although it may be predictable from the consequent distortion or damage. Bowing might be a sign of loss of integrity between masonry leaves, and vertical or diagonal cracking at junctions between internal and external walls might suggest a lack of bond. The distortion survey (Chapter 10) can be planned to give warning, as far as possible, of such hidden deterioration.

Summary

The visual inspection provides part, often the most important part, of the primary evidence, and produces a short list of potential causes. The short list is used to plan the distortion survey and ground investigation which will complete the testing evidence.

Chapter 10

DISTORTION SURVEY

The object of a distortion survey is to measure the departure of walls and floors from the vertical and horizontal planes in which they were built.

Level surveys

The simplest distortion survey would be to take levels on the same brick bed course at each corner of the building. If three corners are at the same level while the fourth is lower, there would be grounds for suspecting subsidence at the fourth corner. That would be a simplistic interpretation, however, the main objection to which is that part or all of the imagined movement could be inherent. If we are to make sense of distortion surveys we must come to terms with built-in distortions.

BS5606 includes a survey of building tolerances. Bricklaying, for example, has a standard deviation of 5.1mm in 3m. In other words 68.27 per cent of walls are laid to that accuracy or better. There is nothing, however, to be gained by applying statistics to the individual case. We need to make a judgement about tolerances on the building under inspection, and this is best done by surveying it accurately and making the best possible estimate of the true original tolerances.

The level survey readings should always be taken on the top of the brick (Figure 10.1), this being the surface which was adjusted to the bricklayer's string line. Readings should be taken using a staff marked with divisions of 1mm or less and sight lines should be short enough to guarantee reading to within 1mm. Change points should be firm and reliable, and the survey should close at its starting point to an accuracy of at least 2mm. That is the minimum accuracy which should be aimed for, if results are to be reliable, and it can be achieved using any standard well-maintained optic level. Higher accuracy can be attempted, but with little gain, with more sophisticated equipment.

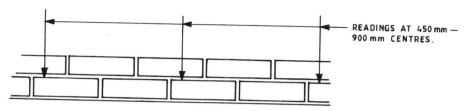

Figure 10.1 *Position of level readings*

Where one wall abuts another, without bond, a reading should be taken immediately on either side of the junction in order to reveal any inherent step at this point (Figure 10.2). Readings should always be continued below window openings. This is easily done by using a boat level as shown in Figure 10.2. At doors, a reading should be taken at either side of the opening, right next to the frame.

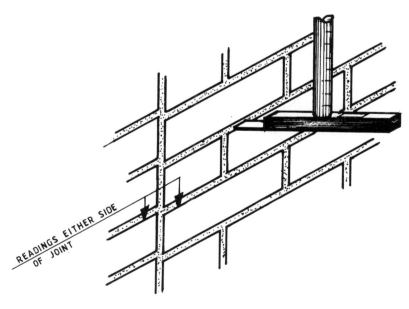

Figure 10.2 *Levelling procedure*

The advantage of frequent and accurate reading is that the inherent variations are displayed by the wobble on the diagram (Figure 10.3). Of course this would not detect every bricklaying inaccuracy. An inherent slope sometimes gets built (especially to extensions) and is not easy to detect. If quirks like that are suspected it may be worth repeating the levelling on a higher brick course, and checking window frames, to see if they were bedded on a tapered mortar joint to get them level.

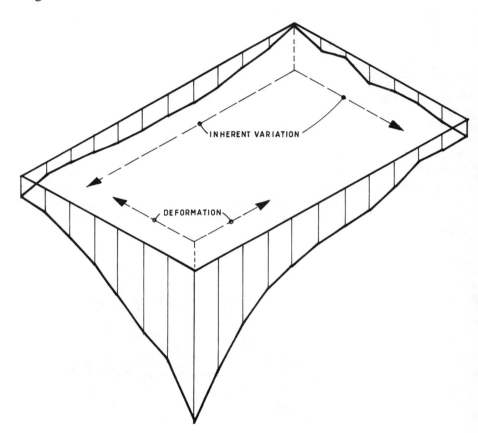

Figure 10.3   *Level survey diagram*

Inherent variations

Readings are best taken at a position at which the bricklayer is likely to have felt comfortable and well sighted, and therefore less likely to stray from the string line. Referring to Figure 10.4: accuracy is least at the top of foundation level (1), where the unevenness of the concrete may take three or four brick courses to iron out. There is usually an improvement at and above damp-proof course level. Above window sill level, the brick gauge may be inaccurate at small piers (2) and above opening heads (3) where readjustment to frame sizes may be attempted by thick bed courses. Between heads and sills (4), continuity improves accuracy provided access is comfortable. If awkward scaffold lifts or other difficulties of access mean that bricklaying has to be done overhand or below knee level or above chest level (say, 5) there can be renewed loss of accuracy which is often more noticeable in the vertical plane. Loss of verticality can occur within the gable apex (6), where the bricklayer may have to adjust to the roof verge. Variable thickness of bed courses (7) betray high inherent variations.

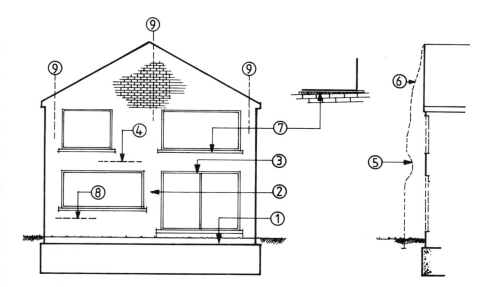

Figure 10.4 *Inherent variations*

With most buildings, the area which combines ease of level reading with reasonable bricklaying accuracy is usually found just below ground floor window sill level (8). Verticalities should be taken both at corners and remote from corners, and are usually most informative at positions where the brickwork is vertically continuous (9).

The inherent variations of stonework are more difficult to eliminate. It is the variation in unit size more than the awkwardness of laying large units which increases the built-in tolerances. Ashlar usually provides a reliable reference. Coursed rubble is often too variable for a useful level survey, although verticality readings usually remain valid. Flint and pebble and other small stone walls often have stringer courses, or plinths, or bands of brickwork which can be used for the level survey, and quoins which can be used for the verticality survey.

Since the main purpose of the level survey is to establish whether there has been foundation movement, one obvious consideration should override thoughts about accuracy and comfort: readings should be taken at a level where the potential distortion will be recorded. Brickwork above damage (Figure 10.5) is often undistorted.

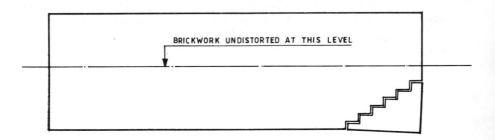

Figure 10.5   *Survey line missing distortion*

The effect of inherent variation is reduced by accurate reading, but never eliminated and never exactly calculated. At the end of the day, a judgement has to be made.

Interpretation

As a general guide to interpretation, a succession of readings which deviate from the plane by only small random amounts would imply that no significant movement has occurred. Foundation movement causes either a tilt or a shear or bending strain (Figure 9.2). A tilt is easily spotted, and is usually accompanied by a low level of damage. Bending shows angular distortion and is reflected by tapering damage. Shear is less easy to detect because damage is caused by relatively low levels of movement.

External brick level surveys are most useful on two or three storey buildings. Pierced walls of bungalows are damaged at very low levels of movement, which may hardly show up on the level survey. Tall buildings are more likely to tilt or shear in response to foundation movement, and again the results are not always vivid enough to overscribe inherent variation.

For buildings with plan areas up to 100m^2, the level survey diagram usually gives a rough idea of overall differential movement. In other words, differential movement should equal highest reading minus lowest, with a reduction for inherent variation. In larger buildings, terraces or blocks of flats, for example, the accumulative tolerances destroy any chance of establishing differential movement, although angular distortion should still be easy enough to detect.

Repeating the distortion survey on different elements increases the chance of obtaining compatible evidence.

Internal levels

Internal levels can be taken on the ground floor. If this is independent of the main foundations it should behave differently from them in response to local shallow movement but probably similar to them in response to a deep-seated movement. These aspects can help interpretation.

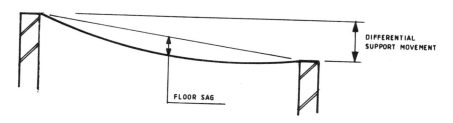

Figure 10.6 *Floor level survey*

Levels on suspended floors will demonstrate differential movement of supporting walls, as well as their own deflection (Figure 10.6). They may detect unwise alterations. Figure 10.7 shows a case where a supporting wall was removed, leaving the floor load to be carried on a timber plate which, although large in section, was not intended to span the full width of the building, and it therefore suffered gross distortion. When the plate was exposed, it was seen to be on the point of failure. Ground floor and first floor levels can sometimes be taken in a single excercise by placing the level first on the ground floor and then on the ceiling above.

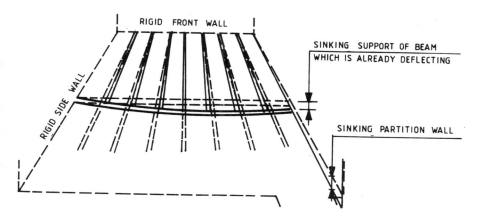

Figure 10.7 *Distortion caused by alteration*

Verticality readings

The vertical profiles of external walls can be measured by theodolite sighting on a scale held perpendicular to the face. Accuracy is as important as with levels, in fact more so. The line of sight must be truly vertical, and the reading must be truly perpendicular to the face. Slight deviation of either is fatal. As with levels, inherent variations have to be judged for the individual case (Figure 10.4).

Some sites are too cramped for a theodolite to operate efficiently. An alternative is a pole-mounted laser which can be raised up the face of the building, sighting on a scale at ground level. Again, a truly vertical line is essential, and the laser beam must be narrow enough to give an accurate reading from the top of the wall.

Verticality readings should be taken at close centres (300mm maximum), partly to eliminate the inherent variations but mainly to record the profile in detail, which is essential to interpretation (Figure 10.8). At its simplest, the verticality survey may confirm subsidence previously suspected from the pattern of cracking and level survey. (It may not always do so if the movement has been a shear deformation rather than tilt or bending.) But it may do more; it may give the strongest of all distortion evidence. Roof spread has a characteristic profile (Figure 10.8 could be roof spread); so does the distortion caused by consolidation or sulphate attack. Terraces sometimes suffer longitudinal creep distortion after many cycles of normal expansion and contraction, which can be detected by the lean of their gable ends. Long unbraced roofs may sway at gables.

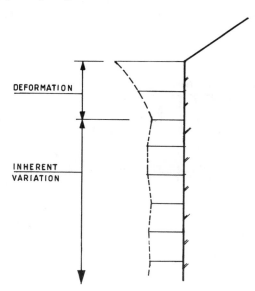

Figure 10.8　*Verticality profile*

Projections such as balconies and bay windows, and difficulties of access, sometimes prevent verticality surveys from being taken at the most informative positions. Readings can be taken on the wall's internal face to avoid these problems, but with some loss of accuracy unless decorations can be removed to expose the masonry, and of course floorboards then have to be removed to allow vertical continuity.

A verticality survey is a good indicator of stability, in two ways. It points to the likelihood of the wall having departed from cross walls and floors, thereby losing restraint, and it measures leans and bulges. It is generally accepted that lightly loaded well restrainted brickwork can lean or bulge by up to 85 per cent of its thickness. Even poorly restrained brickwork can lean by up to 50 per cent and it is nearly always possible to improve poor restraint. In the case of cavity walls the thickness should be taken, for the purpose of judging stability, as that of the thinnest leaf.

Survey time

Distortion surveys can be carried out by anyone competent with surveying instruments. The following times are typical for an irregular shaped two storey building with a ground floor area of 100m^2, and reasonable access all round:

• measuring ground floor layout	1 man 1 hour
• producing outline sketch	1 man 1.5 hours
• external brick course survey	2 men 1 hour
• producing diagram	1 man 1.5 hours
• internal ground floor level survey	2 men 1 hour
• producing diagram	1 man 2 hours
• internal first floor level survey	2 men 1 hour
• producing diagram	1 man 2 hours
• verticality survey (15 readings)	2 men 2 hours
• producing diagram	1 man 2 hours

Roughly 20 man-hours would therefore provide a comprehensive distortion survey for a fair-sized commercial or domestic masonry building. In simple cases, not every exercise would be necessary. In complex cases, extra time would be needed to display and interpret all the results.

Disguised distortion

If the distortion readings have to be taken on a covering (for example, verticality readings on render, level readings on floorboards) then not only are inherent variations greater, but there is a risk that structural distortion has been disguised. This might be unhelpful or helpful. In the case illustrated by

Figure 10.7, considerable relevelling of the floor using wedges and packing pieces had given the impression that distortion was minimal. The ceiling had also been replaced (hung from new ceiling joists) but fortunately its part removal allowed the floor joist soffits to be levelled and this gave the game away. Figure 3.21 showed an example of disguised floor distortion.

A helpful example of disguise was provided by a Victorian building whose back addition had suffered large differential movement (Figure 10.9). Its first floor had been relaid, obviously for some time, and was still level. This suggested that the foundation movement had not recently been active.

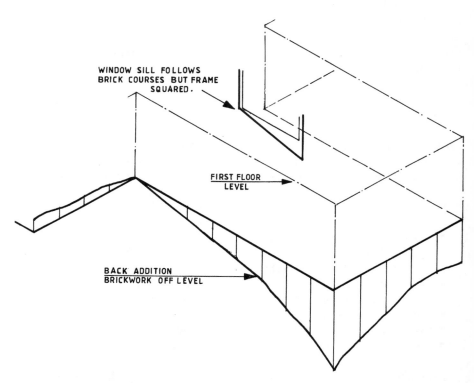

Figure 10.9   *Historic distortion*

Simple distortion surveys

A person working alone can produce a level survey using a water-bottle level, and a verticality survey using a plumb bob hoisted on a pole. There would be no overall saving in time because these processes are clumsier, and, furthermore, some loss of accuracy would have to be accepted.

Pinning a string line to the perimeter brickwork is another alternative to taking individual readings. Photographed using a medium-focal lens, the result can occasionally look spectacular. Even a spirit level can give clues. There are many ways a distortion survey can test theories about damage, even when only crude equipment is available. The case illustrated in Figure 10.9 could have been investigated by using a spirit level on floors and walls, and by observing that window sills were off level, but window frames were square.

A spirit level may reveal the abnormal deflection of an inadequately supported partition, or the racking of a door frame in an internal partition which is subsiding, or the personal problems of a bay window.

Plan distortion

Distortion of the plan shape can be caused by slope instability (Figure 6.10) or lateral heave (Figure 6.6), assuming in the former case that movement is not quick enough to make a distortion survey superfluous. Figure 10.10a shows lateral pressure which could cause distortion. Offset measurements (Figure 10.10b) may detect a bow at right angles to the pressure. On the whole, though, plan distortions are the least rewarding to measure, because the movements, which are usually small, are too easily masked by ill-defined resistance from soil on the other side of the footings, or from the ground floor, or other restraints. Figure 10.10c shows the possible effect of lateral pressure on a retaining wall, and this is, in most cases, easier to detect by verticality measurements.

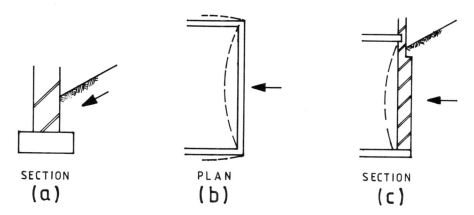

SECTION
(a)

PLAN
(b)

SECTION
(c)

Figure 10.10 *Plan distortions*

Mediaeval buildings

When it comes to mediaeval timber frame, recent distortions tend to be overshadowed by the historic, and surveys are usually more speculative. It can nevertheless be sometimes useful to measure the actual deflection of floors, to separate support movement from floor deflection, and a verticality profile can help to detect incipient instability.

Chapter 11

TESTING

Load testing is generally limited to gravity loading and to only part of the building, and the most common application is to floor areas. Testing may be the most practical way to obtain reassurance that a fire or accident has not caused permanent weakening. It may also be used to prove the strength and stiffness of an existing detail or structure, or of some improvement which has been made to it. Compared with the alternative of structural calculation, it is expensive but more accurate, and sometimes more hopeful. Calculation has to simplify the structure and make cautious assumptions about the quality of the materials, whereas testing circumvents these pessimistic tendencies.

The first step is to decide what load will occur in use. Values for imposed loads are given in British Standards and in the absence of precise information these would normally apply. Surveys on buildings in use have shown, however, that actual loads are often below those listed in the Standards, much lower in some cases, and there is no reason why this information should not be applied carefully, and with safeguards if necessary. (It should obviously not be applied to private houses and other buildings whose future ownership or use cannot be predicted.) The test should take the adopted imposed loads into account, together with an appropriate margin of safety and any dead-weight which is not going to be present during the test.

The margin of safety may take into account dynamic effects which are seldom easy to duplicate in a test. Rarely is it necessary, to do so, but certain cases, such as cantilever balconies or large floors to be used for social functions, have a natural frequency within the expected range of dynamic loading. These should always be checked first by structural calculation, which will quickly establish whether there is a potential problem. If there is, the client can choose whether to avoid it (by stiffening the floor) or confront it (by testing it to establish its true performance).

The first practical consideration is safety. During testing, there is always a risk of unexpected damage or collapse. Behaviour under test load should be predicted and compared with actual behaviour as the test proceeds cautiously, each load increment being delayed until the effects of the previous one have died down. It may even be worth considering fully supporting each increment on jacks so that its application can be made slowly and under complete control. Controlled application would also be a wise precaution if it were necessary, say in the case of an historic building, to limit damage to the absolute minimum.

However good the control, the possibility of collapse should always be considered. Should it occur it must not be allowed to injure anyone or cause damage or instability to other parts of the building. This may mean putting up a safety platform designed to support at least twice the possible weight of debris, twice being the factor required for sudden application, but with an additional allowance for impact if the debris would be falling from any significant height. The procedure itself should be as simple as possible. Loading is usually best applied by small kentledge such as house bricks, and deflections are read by dial gauges supported independently of the tested structure.

The maximum load and number of increments is a decision which should be taken on the merits of each individual case, and the advice of an experienced structural engineer is normally sought. Typically, the load is applied in about ten increments up to the value chosen for the imposed load, including any dead load not already in place. After the structure has sustained this load for a period of time, it is removed and the structure is checked for permanent distortion. The load is then reapplied up to 25 per cent (or whatever figure is chosen) above the imposed load.

Spurious results may arise from secondary effects: bedding down; temperature changes; disturbance of dial gauges; and load sharing. Bedding down is the once-only strain which happens when the first significant loads find their way through the structural members, crushing bits of grit and overcoming incidental friction. A building which has been in regular use is not likely to bed down, but an improvement or alteration might do. If bedding down is likely, it is best to get it out of the way by starting the test normally but unloading when about 50 per cent of the imposed load has been reached, then starting again.

Old floors are often loose at their bearings (loose bearings rather than undersized joists are often responsible for alleged springiness). It would make sense to carry out permanent re-seating or tightening up before applying any test load.

Temperature change can usually be ignored for indoor tests. If in doubt, however, the temperature should be checked at each load increment and if some effect on the stucture's distortion is suspected, it could perhaps be studied by repeating cycles up to the imposed load to see how it varies under similar loads but different temperatures. Alternatively, or additionally, the structure could be observed without load through temperature variations.

Dial gauge supports should be free from interference or accident or, of course, temperature effects. The use of many gauges would help eliminate spurious results and, as an insurance against calamity, it might be worth taking readings by surveyor's level to an accuracy of 1mm, at critical points of the test.

The benefits of load sharing may well be what the test is hoping to prove. But unforseen load sharing would give falsely optimistic results. For example, if the floor under test supports a partition, the latter may, if it is in good contact with the floor, act as a girder, reducing floor deflection and even increasing its capacity. That may or may not matter. But it must be taken into account. It may be possible to sever any connection between floor and partition, and so eliminate its unpredictable effect or, if that is not practical, perhaps the connection should be made more positive so that it can always be relied upon. That, of course, assumes its permanence. When unwarranted load sharing cannot be eliminated, its influence should be reduced by testing as large an area as possible. In the absence of a partition or any other stiffener, load sharing is considered minimal if the loaded width equals the span.

Testing is normally carried out only when there is an excellent chance of success. Nevertheless, failure, whether defined as lack of capacity or unacceptable distortion or damage, is always a possibility. It will be doubly disappointing if any strengthening necessary to bring the structure up to scratch were difficult or ruinous to the appearance of the building. An alternative to abandoning hope might be to regulate the loading of the building when it is re-opened for use. The layout might be altered, swapping heavily loaded areas for light ones. Personnel access might be restricted, if that is the problem, or storage might be limited by permanent barrier.

It goes without saying that load tests should not be relied upon if deterioration cannot be avoided. And if distortion is the problem, some estimate for creep should still be made.

Laboratory testing

Chemical tests are available for measuring mortar constituents, including calcium sulphoaluminate, which is produced by sulphate attack. Bricks can be analysed for their constituent or extraneous salts; wood and roots can be identified by family (individual species cannot be identified; for example poplar and willow cannot be separated). *In situ* or laboratory tests are available for checking strength after fire. Fire intensity, which gives an indirect measure of strength loss, can sometimes be deduced from samples. These tests are all straightforward. If no in-house expertise is available, it is best to discuss the problem with a testing laboratory before obtaining and delivering the specimens. The laboratory will be able to explain the purpose and limitations of various possible tests, and may give useful advice on sampling.

Calculation

There is no *in situ* test for the effects of temperature and moisture change, but simple arithmetic using values supplied by British Standards is enough to show whether the scale of damage is of the order that might be expected. That would only be a crude check, of course. It would be assuming that the cracked element was fully restrained against its potential movement and possessed no tensile strength. A more sophisticated calculation would have to consider the true effect of restraints and tensile capacity.

The same comments apply to shrinkage. However, there is an additional difficulty. The case under consideration is likely to be abnormal shrinkage, caused by materials being unusually wet or green when built-in. There is no way of establishing initial dimensions. We are hampered again by not being able to apply statistics to the individual case.

Calculation for dynamic floor loading has already been mentioned. It is less accurate than static calculation and therefore has to be even more conservative.

Chapter 12

GROUND INVESTIGATION

Testing comes into its own below ground level. If ground conditions appear to be complex, or if refurbishment is going to lead to a considerable redistribution of foundation loads, it will normally be necessary to commission a ground investigation by geotechnical engineers, and this will include a number of *in situ* and laboratory tests. The ground investigation needs as much planning as the rest of the work. An existing building, especially if occupied, is likely to frustrate the ideal investigation. It may prevent the use of certain equipment. A realistic schedule should therefore be made for exploration, sampling and testing, and the work should be supervised by someone with authority to adapt it to suit conditions found.

Ability to adapt is particularly important. The cost of standing time while an obstruction is broken out or a service cable circumvented will add considerably to the estimated cost, to no one's benefit. A two-stage investigation would reduce these risks. The first stage would be superficial, exploratory, and without costly equipment. Part of its aim would be to plan the second stage and to clear any obstructions to drilling and probing.

The purpose of the second stage would be to define any problems which may be known only in general terms, and to assist in predicting the performance of existing foundations (as well as any new ones) after alterations. In certain cases that would call for a calculation of incremental settlement and its effect on the superstructure, which requires a higher order of expertise than designing for new work.

When the purpose of appraisal does not extend beyond finding defects, a more modest ground investigation is usually sufficient. It will normally consist of hand-dug trial holes, shallow boreholes and simple testing. The first trial hole should be positioned to expose a likely defect, using the pattern of damage and other circumstantial evidence as a guide. If the distortion survey has been done it may already be pointing at the source of the building's problems. Whatever prompts the decision on location, there must be a logical reason for it because trial holes are too expensive to speculate. The progress of ground investigation then depends on the suspected defect.

Granular soil and made ground

Subsidence caused by leaching or erosion in made ground or natural granular soil will be characterized by a zone of loosened material. This may be recognized by the ease of digging or by tapping a bar into the ground to feel its resistance. Formal testing is more informative although, as we shall see, too much should not be claimed for it.

If the suspected cause of subsidence is leaking drains, these should obviously be tested. The simplest method is to stop the pipe or pipes at a convenient manhole, charge the upstream length with water and measure the loss over a period of time. The length under test should be filled, but put under the least possible head, because the object is only to check whether it leaks during working conditions, not to test it to destruction. It is usually the connections between the building and first manhole that give most trouble. If these cannot be water-tested, a closed circuit television survey can be carried out by a specialist firm. The survey would detect and describe cracks and deformations in the pipe and its joints, and would enable a decision to be made about the most appropriate means of repair. For example, rejointing and relining are options which may be considerably more economic than replacement, but they cannot be recommended without visual evidence. Not all visual surveys are efficient with pitch-fibre materials, because they may be too dark to register. Lastly, the camera will not, obviously, proceed past blockage or collapse.

Some, but not all, Water Authorities will check for mains water leakage and advise interested customers. In the absence of such a test, collected water may be tested for chlorine content which is higher in mains water than in ground water or drains. The water has to be fresh because the chlorine content is short lived.

When the cause of subsidence has been identified it should be eliminated. The problem will not always end there, however. The ground will continue to consolidate under self-weight and foundation pressure until it gets back to equilibrium. Equilibrium may be achieved quickly or slowly, according to the severity of the case. If quickly, superstructure repair is simple; if slowly, repair will be more difficult and it may be necessary to consider either strengthening or underpinning the foundations to avoid recurrent and perhaps dangerous movement. To be of any use, then, ground testing must contribute towards a judgement about future consolidation.

Continuous density testing by static or dynamic probing will define the depth of loosened soil beneath foundation level, and its extent in plan. This was briefly discussed in Chapter 6. But before discussing testing in more detail, it is worth emphasizing the point about accurate trial hole location. This is more critical in sand or granular made ground than in other types of soil.

In sand which would be naturally dry, a prolonged point leak, such as might occur at a damaged sewer joint or holed water main, can loosen the ground to a considerable depth within a small radius. Beyond the small radius, there may be little or no evidence of looseness. That would be the normal pattern, in fact, since the natural path for escaped water is straight down unless there happens to be a high water table or a layer of impermeable soil at shallow depth. It makes ground investigation difficult. If the worst conditions are not found, the severity of the problem may be underestimated. If the loose conditions are missed altogether, the cause of damage may be incorrectly diagnosed.

With a local deep ground problem, there is simply no guarantee that the worst conditions will be found, unless the investigation is carried out without any respect for normal cost constraint. Experience and logic improve anticipation.

Returning to the subject of testing: the simplest density test equipment is the Mackintosh Probe, a hand-held version of the standard penetration test. Its main benefit to investigation is that it will detect pockets of loose soil or soft layers, such as peat, within a sequence of soils. A small bullet-shaped head is driven into the soil by a hammer of standard weight falling through a standard distance. Because of its low energy, compared with the standard penetration test, the Mackintosh Probe only gives truly comparable data, which may be needed for establishing bearing pressure or settlement if proposed refurbishment would add loading to existing foundations, in silt, sand and weak chalk. It does not efficiently penetrate stiff or dense material, and in soil containing more than five per cent of gravel-sized or larger particles there is a danger that impact energy may be dissipated on an individual particle, giving the impression that the soil is denser than it really is. Within these limits, however, the tool is reliable and useful.

It may be worth mentioning in passing that soils which are naturally loose may, even when undisturbed, show a decrease in resistance (in other words a drop in blow count) a short distance below foundation level. Figure 12.1 shows an example. This apparent loosening is due to the fact that the building load will have consolidated the soil immediately beneath the foundations, and at that level it will now be more dense. A little deeper, the soil will not have benefited to the same degree. Testing would reflect this by showing that the ground was at first becoming somewhat looser with depth, but that should not be taken as an indication of subsidence.

The Mackintosh Probe indirectly measures density by giving a blow count. Blow count is defined as the number of blows required to make the head penetrate by 300mm. This value can be related by charts to bearing pressure.

When carrying out a ground investigation for new buildings, testing leads fairly simply to estimates for bearing pressure and settlement. Inexact problems, such as self-consolidation of made ground, are usually handled by

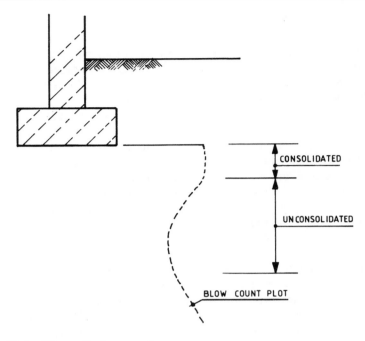

CONSOLIDATED

UNCONSOLIDATED

BLOW COUNT PLOT

Figure 12.1   *Naturally loose soil*

ground treatment or special foundations. With an existing building, inexact problems cannot be evaded.

Beneath a subsiding building, soil movement has two separate causes: bearing pressure and consolidation under self-weight. Probing measures directly only bearing pressure. If an estimate of further movement is made on bearing pressure alone, it will neglect the consolidation under self-weight, which could be much larger. If total movement is to be predicted, a separate judgement for both increments is required.

Settlement due to bearing pressure can be calculated by a geotechnical or structural engineer using standard methods. Estimates of consolidation under self-weight are harder, and probing can only give an indication of severity.

The first step in estimating self-weight consolidation is to establish or assume the extent in plan of disturbed ground. Formal establishment requires probing at close centres round the perimeter foundations. In many cases, the circumstances are sufficiently clear cut to allow a restricted investigation. If even restricted probing is too costly or impractical, a less accurate assessment of the extent in plan would have to be made on the strength of the distortion survey and any other evidence.

A Mackintosh Probe test should be carried out at the worst position, when this is established, and compared with at least one probe taken in undisturbed ground. The test itself should proceed cautiously, not with pre-set increments of 300mm or whatever, because that would obscure important variations. After gently bedding the head at foundation level, the blows should be applied slowly, and the penetration measured after every ten. Occasionally, the head runs away under the impact of a single blow, suggesting the presence of a void (or possibly quicksand conditions), and the size of the apparent void should be measured.

Results are translated easily from penetration to equivalent blow count. For example, successive penetrations per ten standard blows of 150mm, 80mm and 20mm would translate into an equivalent running count of 20, 37.5 and 150. Then, using the results in undisturbed ground as a comparison, a best estimate of future consolidation can be attempted. A void can be assumed to collapse and cause the equivalent amount of subsidence. Otherwise the equivalent running blow counts can be taken as a qualitative indication of looseness and the judgement of future movement can be guided by considering how a similar material would behave as fill.

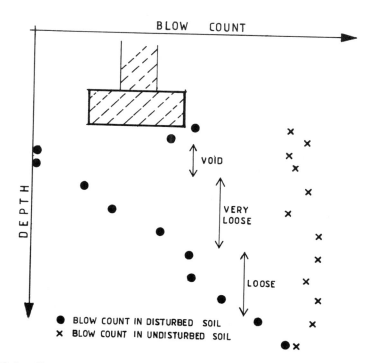

Figure 12.2   *Comparing probe results*

An example is shown in Figure 12.2. Supposing the material would, if loosely tipped, consolidate by five per cent of its thickness, and supposing there are no other factors to take into account, such as degradation, then a rough calculation would proceed as follows: there is a 75mm void, 500mm of very loose material and 600mm of loose material. Taking the very loose as acting like loosely tipped material, and taking loose as having half that effect, there is a predicted movement of $75 + 25 + 12 = 112$mm. This cannot be given as an accurate estimate because it makes crude assumptions, ignores the fact that the loosened ground will almost certainly stabilize before it reaches the density of the undisturbed ground (since the latter nearly always has a margin of safety) and does not take into account the capacity of the building to reduce its movement by redistributing loading. Having made the crude calculation for consolidation, with something added for settlement, and having made some judgements about the building's behaviour, the investigator is left with a feel for the severity of the problem, and that is about as close as one can get without monitoring. Some feel for creep should also be fed into the judgement.

Clay

The two main problems in clay are settlement under load and volume change independent of load. Settlement absorbs more design energy but is the less common complaint, since it is a process which is usually complete within a few years at the very most. So it is a new building problem, and not so many new buildings nowadays, have abnormal settlement for a defect. Settlement can of course be regenerated by adding to the original loads, or by long-term softening of the ground. The latter is rare.

   If settlement is suspected, the theory can be initially tested by taking a number of cohesion values at and below foundation level, using a hand-held vane test in an augered borehole. The average value is then applied (with greater weight given to values nearest to the contact between footing and soil) to one of the standard formulae, which use a factor of safety of three. If the permissible bearing pressure is above the actual bearing pressure, settlement is very unlikely to be a problem. The factor of safety can be taken as a guarantee against abnormal settlement. If the factor of safety is lower than normal, settlement may be a problem and should then be calculated. Calculation is most reliable if based on consolidation tests carried out in a soils laboratory using undisturbed samples. This would demand a specialist investigation. A rough calculation can be made by an engineer, without laboratory testing, by assuming a relationship between cohesion values and soil modulus. The other common clay problem, volume change independent of building load, was mentioned in Chapter 6.

   In areas where heave operates, the first thing to establish is whether the movement is up or down, heave or subsidence. Investigations have not always been correct on this fundamental point, although the success rate has improved since both perils have enjoyed insurance cover. Except for seasonal movement of shallow foundations, the majority of heave/subsidence damage is caused by trees. Growing trees cause subsidence; removed trees cause heave. The latter are not as easy to spot. Their stumps may still be there, unless they were built over, and their roots will certainly still be there, although they are not bound to be revealed by trial hole or borehole. Aerial photographs may be able to prove the previous existence of vegetation, although it is an expensive search without a reasonable forecast of dates.

It may be necessary to demonstrate the presence of roots, dead or alive, below foundations, and to prove where they came from. It is not enough to refer to the National House Building Council's Practice Note 3. The great majority of tree root spread is less than the limits given in the practice note, a necessary condition for any design guide, but there are occasions when the roots can go further. The Kew root survey (described in *Tree Roots and Buildings* by Cutler and Richardson, 1989) established a statistical relationship between tree distance and damaged building for a number of common species, based on case history. But for the individual case, there is no alternative to digging trial holes at the edge of the building and hoping to be lucky. The more likely locations for roots may be forecast by the distortion survey, especially in heave cases, and by site conditions. On dry sites, for example, roots go deeper. In the case of glacial sand and gravel capping shrinkable clay on high ground, few root ends will be found in the sand and gravel, and these would be irrelevant to any damage, and it would normally be necessary to dig a reasonable depth into the clay.

The exact position of any root samples should be recorded. An arboriculturalist can identify specimens by comparison with standard examples under microscopic examination, and can advise on whether the root is dead or alive. Sometimes it is useful to match root with stump. Material from any part of a tree will serve for identification. (Timber from a beam or joist can also be identified, if this is useful in estimating properties like strength and stiffness.) Specimens for identification should be a minimum of 2mm diameter and should not be stored for more than a few hours in plastic bags, because this encourages deterioration. Certain species of tree shed roots seasonally, so a mix of dead and live roots would not necessarily indicate that vegetation has been thinned.

Returning to the question of deciding between heave and subsidence: a minority of problems involve both. The sequence of events which most often leads to their combination is the removal of trees before building (causing heave) followed by the planting of fast-growing water-demanding species afterwards (causing subsidence), both in ignorance of the National House Building Council's Practice Note 3. A mature tree losing vigour can also cause heave. Broken land drains and water bearing seams within the clay can occasionally have unexpected effects.

Local knowledge and visual inspection would tell an experienced observer whether the soil is likely to be shrinkable. Simple testing will provide proof by classification (Figures 6.3 and 6.5). If the clay content appears to be low, it should be measured by a geotechnical laboratory, which will carry out a sedimentation test. The test is not quick. Results usually take about two weeks from delivery of samples.

The samples used for plasticity and particle size distribution can be simply dug or augered out of the ground, because results are not spoiled by disturbance.

If an indication is required of the degree of desiccation, then the moisture content should also be measured in the laboratory. That does require some small preparation. Each sample should be wrapped and sealed in a strong plastic bag as soon as it is taken from the ground. Air should be expelled from the bag to avoid sweating, and samples should be transferred to a cool dark place as soon as possible, and delivered to the laboratory as soon as possible. The low permeability of the clay prevents quick changes in its moisture content and, if these simple precautions are taken, then testing need not begin for 48 hours or so. Additional precautions, if samples have to stand for a weekend, would include using the largest possible pieces of intact clay, double wrapping them and storing them in a room unaffected by central heating or solar gain. Not least important, samples should be clearly identified by marking the outside of the bag.

In a straightforward technical investigation, the most valuable conclusion would be an accurate estimate of future volume changes. If subsidence has occurred, what recovery can be expected when the cause is removed? If heave has occurred, what further movement is to come? Accurate prediction is elusive because many of the factors which influence the answers remain uncertain even after expensive investigation. If more than a very rough estimate is needed, the work should be done by a geotechnical engineer, who would have a better feel than the general practitioner for the accuracy of the calculation in the particular circumstances.

In the case of subsidence, the distortion survey may give a reasonable idea of the amount of previous foundation movement. If simple recovery is to be anticipated, the movement can be taken as equal and opposite to the subsidence, provided the tree is younger than the building. (In practice it may prove to be less.) For heave cases, the distortion survey can give no clue to future movement, and the three most useful ways of estimating volume changes are: swelling tests, effective stress calculation and moisture content profiles.

Swelling tests are carried out on undisturbed samples, although a degree of disturbance is inevitable and will influence results. Water is added to the sample and the swelling is measured. Effective stress calculations can be carried out using pore-pressure readings measured by piezometer. They are beyond the expertise of the general practitioner.

The most convenient method is based on a prediction of the increase of soil moisture content. A moisture content profile is established by taking disturbed samples from a borehole at 300mm centres, starting at foundation level and finishing at a level where desiccation is extremely unlikely. The same borehole should be used for soil classification. The additional tests needed for classification can be carried out on every fourth moisture content sample.

The expected increase in moisture content at each level has then to be calculated. This means estimating the final, or 'equilibrium', moisture content. Several formulae for equilibrium have been suggested, such as $0.5 \times$ liquid limit or (a less logical choice) plastic limit + four per cent, but a more reliable method would be to obtain a moisture content profile on the same site remote from the influence of any existing or previous vegetation, if that is possible.

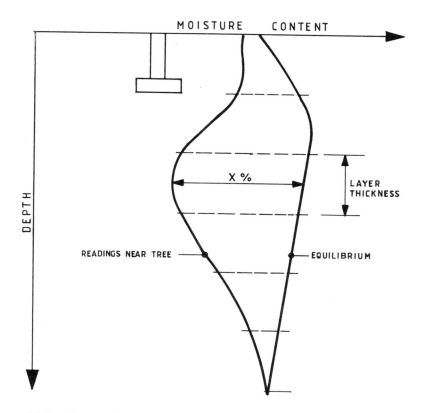

Figure 12.3   *Comparing moisture content profiles*

Figure 12.3 shows a diagram where a tree-affected moisture content profile is compared with a profile at assumed (measured or calculated) equilibrium. At each level, there is an expected increase in moisture content of, say, x per cent. Swelling of that layer would then be: x per cent times the thickness of the layer times a factor.

The moisture content has to be translated from the laboratory test results, which are calculated by weight, to volumetric moisture content, and expressed as a decimal. The laboratory can give the results in volumetric terms, if requested. Normally, this requires one extra test for specific gravity, but bearing in mind the inherent uncertainty of heave calculations, a figure of 2.7 can be assumed in the absence of testing. Taking W as the laboratory moisture content by weight (defined as weight of moisture divided by weight of solid) and expressing it as a decimal, then volumetric moisture content is calculated as $2.7W/(1 + 2.7W)$.

Subtracting existing volumetric moisture content from equilibrium gives an assumed deficiency of, say, Wd at each layer. Vertical heave is roughly one quarter of moisture deficiency, so each layer will increase its thickness by 0.25Wd × original thickness.

Without specialist advice, such a calculation should be used only as a tentative indication of the likely severity of heave. Heave movement of 25mm or less can be accommodated without severe damage. More than 100mm will, unless prevented by underpinning, cause at least serviceability problems and will probably cause serious structural damage. The decision on whether to underpin or wait for recovery can only be based on a prediction of future behaviour, however tentative that prediction may have to be. Potential heave is one part of that prediction; time is another.

The time taken for heave, or recovery, to run its course is even more difficult to estimate than the total movement, because (in southeast England and East Anglia) it is influenced by small changes in the weather. Only rainfall is available to fuel recovery; and run-off, evaporation and transpiration take their toll before there is a useful increase in moisture content in the soil. Long periods can elapse between short bouts of movement. The pattern defies monitoring. There is no artificial way of hastening the process.

In Chapter 6, ten years was mooted as the typical period between onset of damage and virtual inactivity. Where the total movement is likely to be less than 25mm, a shorter period can be hoped for, provided there are no prolonged dry spells and no serious obstructions to rainfall reaching foundation level. In urban areas, where buildings are surrounded by impermeable paving, heave will take much longer to run its course. It may never 'finish', in other words equilibrium may not be achieved, unless the area is redeveloped.

Time is a measure of inconvenience, and it may or may not be an important factor in deciding whether to underpin. Frequent slight damage is more than irritating to house owners, even if the dwelling remains safe. Owners and occupants of commercial or industrial buildings are seldom as concerned about cosmetic damage, but they will be more alarmed by potential delays arising from serviceability damage.

Safety

Supervisors of ground investigations should be well aware of the requirements of the Health and Safety at Work Act. The public should be kept away from excavations, and all excavations should either be back-filled or covered safely at the end of the working day. Unshored excavations deeper than 1.2m should not be entered. Construction personnel are often adept, through practice, at using unsafe methods and equipment, but they should be actively discouraged from bad habits, and if their work seems casual it should be eyed with suspicion. Shored excavations, ladders and scaffolding should not be used uncritically.

When opening trial holes or boreholes, underground services must be expected, especially close to the surface. Location plans provided by others are usually inaccurate. Clues to positions of service runs may be obtained from manholes and surface markers, and positions of entries to existing buildings. But the danger of striking services can never be eliminated. Mechanized drilling equipment should not be used without checking first with a cable detector. Overhead cables can cause death by electrocution if ladders or distortion survey staffs and poles are erected close to them.

Anyone handling soil should be protected against tetanus (unless they are allergic to the serum). Land which is derelict or near a water course may be infected by Weil's disease (also known as leptospirosis), which is spread by rats. The disease is caught through open cuts or by swallowing the water. Made ground may contain many other pollutants, and soil which is warm or of unnatural appearance should not be handled before it has been analysed. Gas detectors should be used if there is a possibility that the made ground can produce methane or other harmful emissions, and this possibility cannot be judged from the nature of the ground near surface level, because gas can travel, from source, through natural ground. If animal remains are uncovered from an unrecorded pit, there is a possibility of anthrax spores being released.

Chapter 13

INTERPRETATION

There is not a set pattern for interpretation. The route it follows is dominated by whether the building is safe and whether the information gathered is adequate for the purpose of appraisal. Most investigations are of safe buildings which yield adequate evidence, in which case the interpretation follows the simple principle, outlined in Chapter 2, of testing every potential cause against each piece of evidence and reaching conclusions by a process of elimination. A surplus of evidence makes for confident conclusions.

Confidence wanes when inadequacy creeps in. Evidence may be inadequate in some local aspect only, and that may be quite tolerable, or it may throw a cloak of doubt over the whole exercise. Decorative coverings hide possible decay or previous damage, but only the most comprehensive appraisal would insist on their removal. In most buildings, at least a proportion of load bearing walls are either uncovered or have coverings old enough to be expressing any recent movement. Given at least that quality of information, the risk of missing significant damage is small and the risk of missing severe damage is very small.

It is a degree more worrisome with mediaeval buildings because their most critical problem is decay, which will not be on view if the timber is covered. Leaving the question of decay in abeyance when it could be so important is hardly a satisfactory qualification to an appraisal, although in most cases even a superficial inspection can lead to a tentative assessment, which can be used as the basis for either estimating risk or else commissioning a wider investigation.

Investigation which is severely curtailed through lack of funds or restriction of access may be too inadequate to identify any cause of damage with confidence. That can hardly ever be satisfactory. There are three possible types of remedy: widen the scope of the investigation; recommend the sort of action which, on the basis of available evidence, would satisfy the worst possible prognosis; or carry out a more intense study within the limits imposed. To the investigator, widening the scope is always preferred. It stands the best possible chance of accumulating enough evidence to reach a firm conclusion.

Coping with the worst possible prognosis would be safe but probably uneconomic. For example, if neither thermal movement nor subsidence can be eliminated as the potential cause of damage, the only safe immediate action would be to underpin and provide movement joints. That may seem a silly example, but it is not an imaginary one. At a more excusable level: suppose the cause proves to be foundation heave on clay soil, but it is impossible to judge whether this heave has a significant lateral component. If underpinning is necessary, a scheme should have to be devised which copes with both the known vertical and the possible lateral heave.

If neither a widened scope of investigation nor a catch-all solution is practical, investigation can only proceed by improving the value of available information. In the case of masonry damage, for example, it is possible to link the cracks to bending or shear strains and, taking into account the geometry of the wall, the behaviour which has led to the damage. If, on the other hand, visual inspection is frustrated, a more comprehensive distortion survey might at least partly fill the gap. Some residue of uncertainty will always remain: brickwork is far from homogeneous; distortions can never be segregated from inherent variations. Evidence from several viewpoints, however unsophisticated, is nearly always more convincing than an intensive scrutiny of narrow information.

Turning to the unsafe category: buildings rarely become unsafe as a result of the common causes mentioned in Chapters 3 to 6. Either they meet an irresistible overload, which even the best constructed building would fail to withstand, or they are abnormally sensitive to normal loading. In either case, the actual failure is always caused by a load. It may be that the most significant event leading up to the overload was the unexpected transfer of forces to a weak and sensitive detail, and there may be some interesting reasons why that happened, but the final incident will always be a load. The investigation must first identify this event and then work away from it to discover the events which led up to it.

Of course, an investigator can be unlucky enough to be inspecting an undamaged building which is on the verge of catastrophe. No one can guarantee to predict failure before it happens, but in some cases there is just enough advance warning of the coming together of unfavourable circumstances to raise the alarm and justify a proper evaluation. The extra work may lead to timely preventive action. For example, recent excavation may be spotted as a potential instigator of ground instability; a sensitive roof may be seen for what it is before any harm is done; or the discovery could be fortuitous. Investigators with wide experience of distortion surveys, especially on old buildings, will testify to the sometimes surprising amount of horizontal movement between different parts of a building on the same level, and this can unexpectedly advertise a serious loss of bearing in a principal beam.

Figure 13.1 shows a sectional detail of a building with a basement beneath part of its ground floor. Over the years one of the basement walls, which was supporting a four storey load-bearing partition, had repeatedly yielded to earth pressure. The occasional crack had been wedged and pointed; the accumulated movement went unnoticed. The partition in danger of losing support was studwork and it survived the occasional jolts very well. Luckily, an investigation eventually connected the distorted decorations at partition ends with renewed basement-wall rotation, and disaster was averted. Had the scale of damage been less, the approaching disaster might not have been anticipated. It is impossible to plan an investigation which will give adequate information for all possible unsafe conditions. No investigation is entirely free of this risk.

The different styles of interpretation are considered in more detail in the next four chapters.

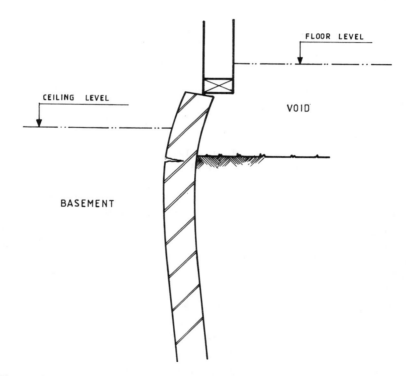

Figure 13.1   *Damage slight: distortion dangerous*

Chapter 14

MASONRY BUILDINGS

With safe, damaged masonry buildings, the main sources of evidence are: visual inspection, distortion survey, and ground investigation; each useful but imprecise. Two very simple examples will show the power of evidence when used in combination.

Within a few months of being built, a chalet bungalow (Figure 14.1) showed cracking in and around its front wall. In particular, its large bay windows separated from the rest of the building. The foul drains running very close to the front wall were found to be leaking severely (even through a manhole base) and were therefore a potential cause. The distortion survey showed, unexpectedly, that the building was leaning away from the front wall. The subsequent ground investigation revealed firm clay at the front and a deep pocket of peat at the rear. Damage formed not at maximum movement but at the weakest part of the structure. Visual evidence alone might have suggested local subsidence caused by leaking drains but in routine combination with other evidence it reliably proved a different cause.

Figure 14.2 shows the corner of a building with a hipped roof and damage which a previous survey had diagnosed as settlement. The level survey discovered no evidence for foundation movement, whereas the verticality survey indicated outward movement at eaves consistent with roof spread. Inspection revealed that hip and jack rafters had not been tied back at this level. The combined evidence was powerful enough not to need a ground investigation for further proof.

Not every case is as simple. Harder cases rely first on accuracy of observation and second on the standard of presentation. Observation has been discussed.

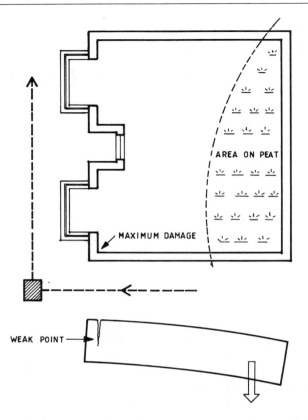

Figure 14.1   *Settlement on peat*

Presentation

Distortion surveys should be produced as diagrams, using an exaggerated scale in the direction of the readings. The level survey need not be strictly isometric. It is more important to choose an angle of view which does not obscure the pattern of distortion, assuming there is a pattern distinct enough to emerge from inherent variations.

Sometimes it is difficult to achieve clarity with three-dimensional presentation. Figure 14.3 is a diagram of levels taken on the perimeter of a commercial development. It proves movement, but the pattern is obscure. Figure 14.4 shows a contour drawing of the same building. This represents a stage of interpretation beyond mere recording, because the contour lines are produced through the interior of the building without justification. If we allow that licence, the contours form a remarkably good fit with the level readings, only one of which was left on the wrong side of a contour. The bold line in Figure 14.4 encompassed nearly all of the observed damage and outlined an

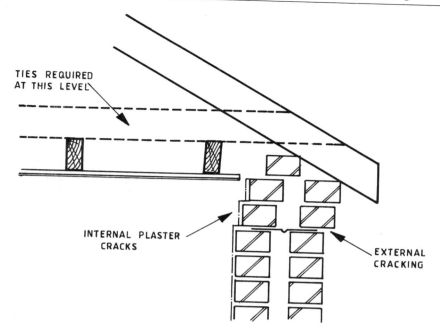

Figure 14.2 *Spread of hipped roof*

area of loose fill which had been causing it.

In most cases, floor distortions are easier to understand from contours than from three-dimensional display. Elderly buildings with internal distortions and damage, probably caused in part by forgotten alterations, may benefit from selected sections showing distortions of both floor and walls (Figure 14.5).

Distortion diagrams are normally reproduced in the report. Having gone to the trouble of preparing them to assist interpretation, they may as well be used to support the commentary, in fact, to replace it to some extent, since a verbal description of distortions has little impact.

Diagrams of damage are also easier to absorb than the usual crack catalogue which even a fellow professional finds turgid. Unfortunately the cost of preparing neat sketches cannot always be justified, but for the purpose of interpretation, at least, the damage should be sketched free-hand on site, using a convention as described in Chapter 9. Without a visual record, the memory fades, and conclusions then rely unwittingly on only part of the evidence. Free-hand sketches are also suitable for discussion with colleagues.

Compatibility of evidence

Returning to compatibility of evidence: interpretation starts with a theory about the cause of damage, drawn from previous experience and a knowledge

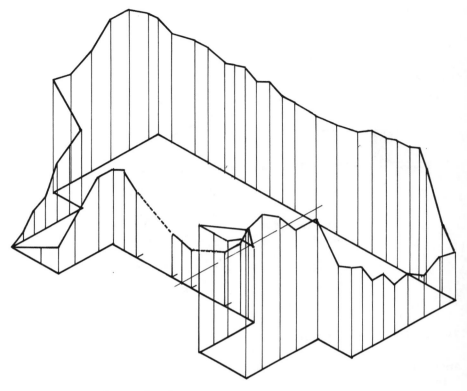

Figure 14.3   *Indistinct level survey*

of typical defects. Its first test is the pattern of damage itself. In the case of masonry, damage is cracking, and cracking is nearly always tensile. It is therefore possible to imagine the movement which has caused it. A crack which is more than hairline represents strain perpendicular to itself and the underlying movement would be either bending or pure elongation. If the crack tapers, or openings distort, this would suggest bending, but not conclusively because a number of factors, such as restraint from floors and cross walls and the difference in behaviour between brick (or stone) and mortar, can deflect a crack from its preferred course.

Displacement along the line of the crack itself would suggest shear deflection. Lipped cracks suggest out-of-plane movement. Cracks which run along and open up a bed course suggest out-of-plane bending.

When there is supporting evidence to come, there is no point in reading everything from the crack pattern. Figure 2.1 showed a very simple case which was capable of more than one interpretation when there was only the visual evidence to go on. At that stage, no feasible explanation for the damage should be discarded. All possible causes should be lined up for checking against the distortion survey.

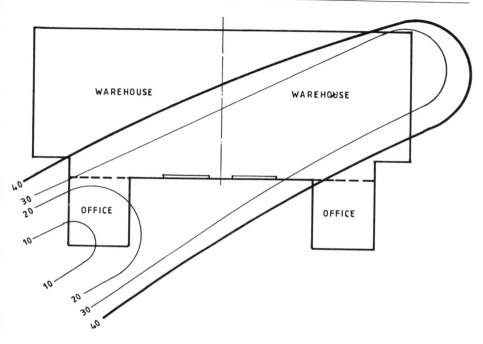

Figure 14.4 *Level contours*

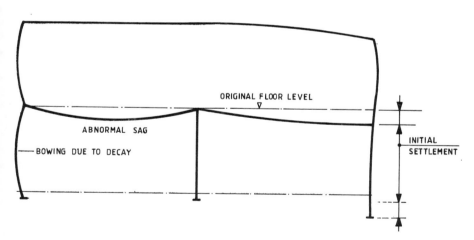

Figure 14.5 *Distortion shown on section*

Distortion surveys are good at detecting tilting, bending, leaning and bulging of walls, and leaning and sagging of floors. They cannot detect elongation, Their usefulness fades where small movement causes notable damage. With these strengths and weaknesses in mind, the distortion survey is used to screen out as many of the inoperable causes as possible. What remains after that test is then tried against the remaining evidence. Ground investigations are essential if any of the remaining potential causes are underground. Desk studies and commonsense supply cheap and effective evidence.

Often the most difficult part of an investigation is deciding what to do. Every case is a compromise between available funds, obstacles to inspection, quality of information and normal value-for-money considerations. The ground investigation can be omitted if visual inspection and distortion survey rule out foundation movement beyond reasonable doubt. On the other hand, if scrutiny fails to focus on a convincing cause, it is a sign that not enough work has been done. That fact may have to be accepted – the investigation may for example be limited by client instructions – in which case interpretation must make the best possible use of available information, stating its limitations and recommending further work.

Distortion compatibility

The distortion survey provides opportunities to test for compatibility within itself. Figure 14.2 showed how the lean of a wall (verticality survey) was shown not to be caused by foundation movement (level survey). Figure 14.6 shows the case of a building whose level survey (a) expressed the same degree of movement as the verticality survey (b), and additional evidence was provided by the floor level survey (c). There could not be any doubt that the building was tilting, with virtually no bending or separation between elements.

Horizontal bed-joint cracking can have a number of potential causes. Supposing the external perimeter level survey finds no significant differential movement of this wall, the verticality survey would be called on to narrow the field. Figure 14.7 shows possible profiles. Case (a) is typical of bulging caused by decay. Inspection should establish the detailed cause. Case (b) could be out-of-plane bending caused by subsidence of a different part of the building. Case (c) is an out-of-plane bending caused by tilting restrained at roof level. These effects are not always captured vividly by the verticality readings, and every cause which remains feasible should be tested against further evidence.

Certain causes have characteristic patterns of distortion. Most types of subsidence involve loss of support immediately beneath part of the foundations (obviously this description excludes mining subsidence and other examples of deep instability). Their effect is shallow and local, and shows up on a level survey. Floors supported on subsiding walls would sink in sympathy but a ground-supported slab would probably remain independent. Heave, on the other hand, whether shallow or deep seated, nearly always affects a ground-supported slab as much as (if not more than) load-bearing foundations.

Damage and distortion are always influenced by the shape and strength of the building. With well built cellular construction, an unexpected force, or loss of support, would be resisted by various wall and floor components acting

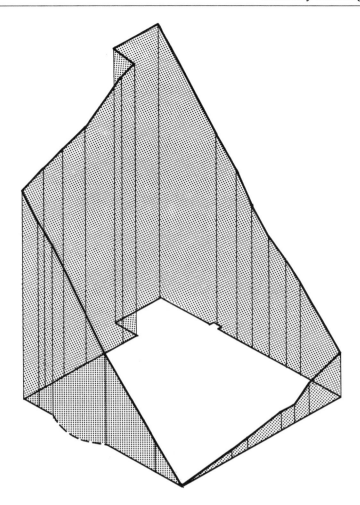

Figure 14.6 (a)   *Distortion compatibility*

together, and damage would probably include torsional disruption. This ability to absorb damage, minimizing but spreading its effect, makes interpretation difficult. A good visual record is all the more essential.

Negative evidence

Negative evidence is no less valuable than positive evidence. Figure 10.9 illustrated the case of a level first floor proving that historic masonry distortion was inactive. Figure 14.8 shows damage to a single-storey office. This appeared in a wall which was 19m long, slightly staggered in plan and with no joints, so movement caused by temperature change was the obvious potential cause. It

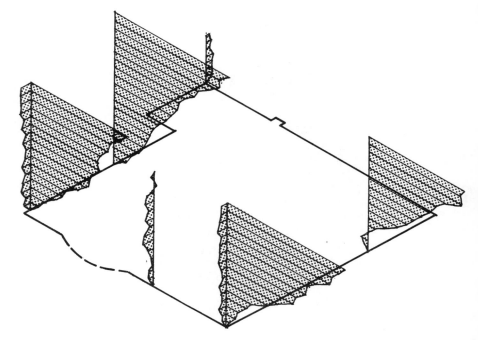

Figure 14.6 (b)

was not necessarily the only one, because the damage had progressed, albeit at a gentle rate, to the level where foundation movement was a genuine alternative. A distortion survey found nothing alarming, but single storey buildings are damaged by small distortions and for that reason level surveys are often inconclusive, so four trial holes were opened for the purpose of testing ground conditions. All was well. The negative evidence was needed to give immediate reassurance and to justify the simple insertion of movement joints.

It is unusual to use trial holes to search for trouble more or less at random. That is an inefficient and risky way to organize a ground investigation, and in most cases the evidence from the visual inspection and distortion survey is good enough to be used as a guide to locating trial holes and boreholes.

Relative importance of evidence

It is difficult to say which of the techniques – visual inspection, distortion survey or ground investigation – is the most important. All are essential (assuming foundation movement is a potential cause and the damage is not self-evidently a local superstructure problem) but one or the other may have the leading role, depending on circumstances. Distortion surveys often provide the most compelling evidence in the case of two or three storey buildings. Figure 14.9

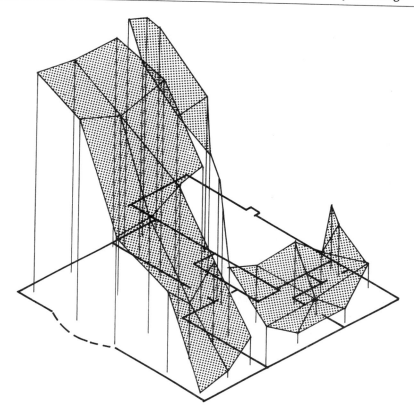

Figure 14.6 (c)

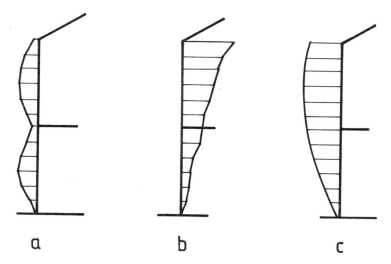

a   b   c

Figure 14.7 *Verticalities*

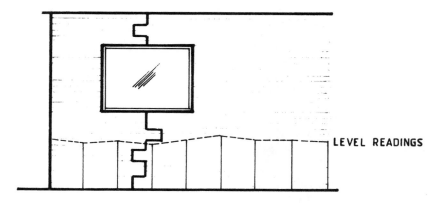

Figure 14.8   *Damage distinguished from movement*

shows an example of an L-shaped two-storey building. Maximum damage occurred at the change in level but its pattern was not in itself demonstrative. The level survey clearly demonstrated upward movement of the smaller wing and the cause was proved to be heave.

Taller buildings need better visual clues. Since their walls are stiffer in bending than in shear, damage is less likely to be deflected far from its source. On the other hand, tilting and shear deflection, the more common forms of damage in tall buildings, emerge less clearly from inherent variations and so appear less spectacular on a distortion diagram. This handicap is often overcome if the distortion survey can be more comprehensive than usual, repeating the perimeter level readings higher up the building, carrying out internal floor-level surveys, and so on.

With bungalows, both the pattern of damage and the level survey are sometimes indistinct, and trial holes are then needed to make sense of the problem. These need careful location, despite, or rather because of, the indistinct evidence. Some guidance may be possible from other sources, such as the onset of damage.

Onset

The onset of damage, that is, its timing, is characteristic of the cause. As a first step, we can distinguish between defects which are built in and defects which are caused by an agent appearing on the scene later. The term 'built in' is not meant to imply negligence in the design or construction, although either might be the case. For this discussion, it simply means congenital defects, and the point is that with few exceptions these all become apparent within the first ten years.

The most important built-in defect is settlement under load. Established buildings have virtually completed their settlement even if they are on poor ground. It may be advisable to restore lost integrity, in other words to stitch

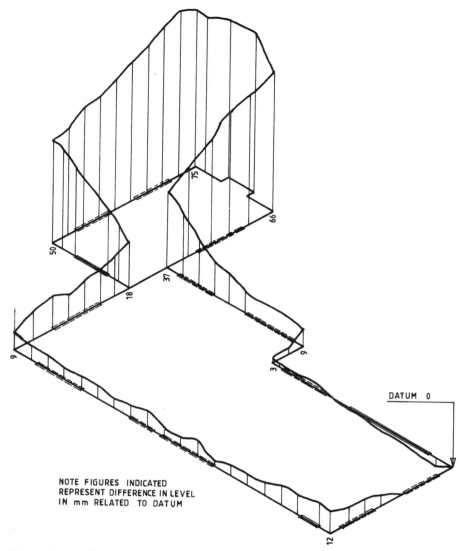

Figure 14.9 *Heave demonstrated by level survey*

cracks and rebond junctions, but there will be no point in arresting extinct movement. Settlement damage can of course be exacerbated or even caused by bad construction. Serious dimensional errors in traditional foundations and faults of detail in modern designed foundations, such as bad connections between piles and beams or bad steelfixing in rafts, would in certain circumstances be prime causes of structural damage. Their effect would be to overload the soil, and as far as timing is concerned, that would usually happen as soon as might be expected from any other type of settlement under load.

(There would be a delayed onset in some cases. For example a weak pile shaft might have to be attacked by ground water before it loses capacity.)

Damage arising from any basic construction fault will normally appear in the first ten years or so. This is worth keeping in mind because many faults have no consequence. A healthy building finds ways to cope. There are of course cases where a fault has some significance in that it represents a weak spot that renders a building more sensitive than in would otherwise have been to whatever afflicts it in later years. That would be significant to the appraisal, but the search for the cause of the current damage would still have to look beyond the mere fault. For example, a poorly restrained wall with mediocre foundations might become damaged after decades of good health; its lack of restraint and the quality of its foundations would influence the nature and severity of damage, but there would have to be a distinct and separate cause, which led directly to the incident and which must be identified.

Typical timing

Drying shrinkage appears in the first year, sometimes lasting into the second if the amount of shrinkage is abnormal. It can recur if internal heating is improved, but would still be short lived.

If thermal or moisture movement is going to cause damage, it should be making its appearance soon after it has gone through a normal expansion/contraction cycle, which is almost certain to occur within the first ten years. (In the case of flat roofs, temperature movement may increase over the years as reflective chippings are blown off.)

Most problems which creep after the initial burst of movement – settlement on peat or made ground, and roof spread, being typical examples – expend most of their energy in the first ten years. Occasional cosmetic damage is all that occurs afterwards. On rare occasions, roof spread remains precariously stable for a long time and then causes serious damage during another incident such as a storm, but most late-life roof spreads are generated by newly covering a badly tied structure. Certain problems such as biodegradable fill can cause damage over a period of decades, although onset usually occurs in the first ten years.

Heave is often misdiagnosed because the agent has gone. It is a pity that its timing cannot, in recompense, be more helpful. When trees are removed from shrinkable clay, there is potential for heave which starts to be realized as soon as the soil moisture content rises. The potential remains until the moisture content has returned to equilibrium. If foundations are constructed before equilibrium is restored, and if the subsequent swelling is powerful enough to cause damage, then this usually becomes apparent in the first ten years. That is the standard case. Unfortunately, there are many non-standard cases and, because of these, onset is not as consistent a clue with heave as it is with other types of foundation movement.

It is well known that dry spells delay onset, or extend its life, but so can other less obvious influences such as impermeable paving and the removal of all stormwater from the vicinity by sealed drains. There is even a small minority of cases which are difficult to attribute at all to trees but seem to have been triggered suddenly by an unexpected water supply. Even in those cases, it is likely that a degree of desiccation existed beforehand, probably caused by a long-forgotten tree.

Settlement under load and 'standard' heave cases are, then, the only built-in problems. Other below-ground problems need an agent, something which appears on the scene later. In one form or another that agent is usually water.

Water can leach granular soils and erode chalk. Its removal can collapse fine soil and shrink shrinkable clay. In each case, onset is determined by the incident, although the delay between cause and effect can sometimes disguise that to a certain extent.

In the case of leaching, considerable energy is required to remove sufficient of the finer particles from the soil matrix to induce collapse under bearing pressure and self-weight. A burst water main can supply this energy very quickly, if it occurs close to the foundations. The energy of stormwater and foul drains depends on their volume and head.

Citing leakage as a cause of damage would be made (partly, never entirely) on the grounds that onset was too late for settlement to be the cause. Technical discussion need not be any more elegant than that. Sometimes, however, a more accurate date of onset is required to establish liability. This usually introduces the chicken and egg question: did subsidence break the drains or did drains cause the subsidence? It is usually fair to say that unless there is evidence of bad workmanship during drain laying, or wear and tear of materials, or a known incident, then fractures close to the building will most likely have been caused by ground movement. Many healthy foundations respond to slight ground strains, moving several millimetres over the years. That need not distress the building, but it is enough, eventually, to cause a shear failure in a pipe, or one of its joints, particularly if a brittle material such as salt glazed ware has been used.

So, in the absence of a distinct cause of drain damage, the probable sequence of drain related damage is: ground strain (or creep) acceptable to the building but not to drains; drain rupture and leakage; leaching of fine particles; building subsidence. Only the last incident is easy to date.

Tree roots are sometimes associated with broken drains. Roots do not invade drains until there is a leak. The leak need not be spectacular. Roots are very efficient at exploiting slight weepage at joints, eventually forcing their way into the interior. Where trees and drains are close to each other, the roots may be powerful enough to pierce or displace drain pipes, and so cause direct physical damage; and of course if the ground is shrinkable clay they may damage the drains by causing them to subside.

Chalk solution is a slow process, difficult to date, although the consequent subsidence may come without warning. The cause, however, is seldom in dispute, so the timing is not critical. Collapse of weak chalk, caused by an increase in moisture content, is usually sudden and therefore easily linked to its cause.

De-watering causes subsidence in silt and peat. The effect is immediate because water which was originally supporting part of the load is removed. Inundation of sand can also cause immediate subsidence. The amount of subsidence is greatest on the first occasion. Repeated inundation has diminishing effect. In the case of clay/tree subsidence, movement occurs soon after tree roots become active beneath foundations.

In all cases of subsidence, damage is delayed until foundations no longer have the strength or stiffness to span across the area of soil affected.

Seasonal patterns

Subsidence due to clay shrinkage occurs most frequently in September and October, although it can be a little earlier or later, according to the weather. Heave recovery is too intermittent always to have a seasonal pattern. On average it is most active in late winter and only likely to persist through summer if the desiccation was severe and the summer is wet. Frost damage is seasonal and this is usually a reliable clue.

Discovery

There is a delay between cause and effect, while resistance to damage is being overcome, and then a delay between the appearance of damage and its observation, and lastly a delay before investigation. During this time, evidence can fade and red herrings can take its place. For example, clay may be dry in late summer, when subsidence occurs, but moist in February when sampled. That may seem too obvious an example, but it has occasionally misled investigations, even when onset of damage was known.

The delay between appearance and observation can be more misleading because it is never known. House owners are the most observant clients but of course if the damage occurs in areas they seldom visit, such as basements, dating onset is still difficult. Commercial building users have a higher threshold of anxiety, and tend to ignore slight damage, especially if it is only mildly progressive.

Figure 14.10 shows the distortion of the front wall of a block of shops and offices. Movement was caused solely by faulty stormwater discharge. The defect had been present for most of the life of the 70-year-old building. When plaster was removed to bond the front walls to cross walls, gaps up to 100mm wide were found to have been filled intermittently during the many redecorations.

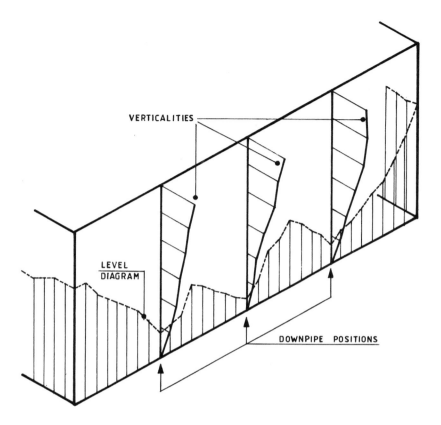

VERTICALITIES

LEVEL DIAGRAM

DOWNPIPE POSITIONS

Figure 14.10 *Disguised movement detected by distortion survey*

Repetition of damage

Foundation problems, by their nature, tend to strike at random and cause a unique pattern of damage. If there is a degree of repetition to the damage, that is, patterns of damage which repeat in similar places, this usually implies a cause which lies purely within the superstructure.

Figure 14.11 shows a section through the stairwell of a large block of flats. Damage consisted of horizontal cracks in the walls near eaves, some ceiling cracking and a slump in the roof outline, as viewed externally. This repeated at each of the four stairwells, and was confined to those areas. The cause was roof spread. The stairwell roofs were not well designed, and they were allowed to apply horizontal loading to walls weakened by large window openings. Within the dwellings themselves, which had trussed rafter roofs, damage was restricted to normal shrinkage cracking at ceiling board joints.

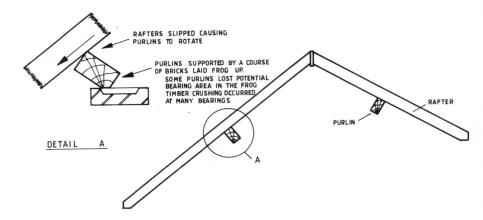

Figure 14.11   *Badly built roof*

Damage classification

It is pointless to consider damage in isolation, without forecasting the likelihood of further movement, but for the purpose of discussion we can take the snapshot view first and talk of further movement later.

The Building Research Establishment has supplied a common classification for damage to low-rise masonry buildings, which has become accepted shorthand and should whenever appropriate be used in reports. Building *Research Establishment Digest 251* describes their classification. Six categories of damage are defined, based on crack width and ease of repair.

A broader classification can be applied to all types of building, using empirical labels: cosmetic damage; serviceability damage; and instability. The first has a nuisance value depending on the aesthetic worth of the building or on how sensitive the market value is to light damage. The second has an inconvenience value. Distortion would be serious enough to rupture pipes or make doors inoperative or cause loss of weather-tightness. Commercial buildings can be disrupted or put out of action by serviceability damage. The third broad category demands immediate attention to prevent local or wholesale collapse.

Categories are of course empirical. Even a slightly damaged building can be precarious, (Figure 13.1), and the investigator must be satisfied that it has sufficient reserves to qualify as safe. That judgement is exercised during the investigation and confirmed during the interpretation. Occasionally, at the latter stage, the investigator will decide to return if the distortion survey gives alarming results or if it seems important in retrospect to uncover a suspect detail. The two most common dangers to apparently safe buildings are local overstress and instability.

Figure 14.12 shows how a combination of historic and current movement, decay and overload, can threaten beam bearings. Damage can also escalate suddenly if, for similar reasons, elements which rely on mutual support are forced apart.

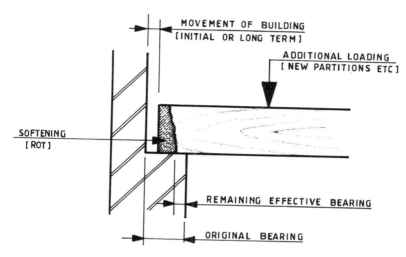

Figure 14.12 *Movement and deterioration*

Safety is threatened by instability rather than crack size. Instability can arise from foundation movement, or wall decay, or overload (usually eccentric), and is characterized by leans and bulges. Chapter 10 discussed acceptable limits, noting that these are partly governed by restraint. A building which exercises good restraint on all its elements is described as robust. Robustness depends on plan shape (Figure 14.13) and on the strength of connections between elements. It can sometimes be threatened if even non-load bearing elements are removed without compensation.

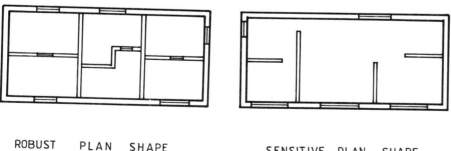

ROBUST   PLAN   SHAPE   SENSITIVE   PLAN   SHAPE

Figure 14.13 *Robustness*

A building which is prone to disproportionate distortion under load or is precariously stable would be described as sensitive. Chapter 17 gives some examples of sensitivity.

Survey reports on old buildings frequently comment on the visually apparent bulges. They rarely notice distortion in new buildings, though the latter are more vulnerable because their two skins are thin, and the outer one relies for its stability on wall ties which traditionally have not enjoyed high standards of workmanship (many buildings have far fewer ties than they should, and not always well fixed) or durability (the life expectancy of ties was discussed in Chapter 5). There is no doubt that modern buildings need the restraint provided by current regulations.

Prognosis

A defect which has run its course is of little concern. That is why it is important to differentiate between settlement which can be relied upon to be old and subsidence which could be new. At worst, an extinct cause will have a legacy of damage and loss of restraint, which can be restored with ease in all but very serious cases.

If the cause remains active, a decision has to be made on how to manage it. There are three options: allow the cause to work its way out on the grounds that its worst effects will be mild; remove the cause and wait for the building to stabilize; or take immediate steps to arrest the problem. If time permits, a period of monitoring will sometimes improve both the efficiency and certainty of remedial action.

To summarize: successful interpretation depends on establishing a theory and testing it against each piece of evidence. It would be inefficient to gather evidence at random, and the investigation usually follows a hopeful trail: the visual inspection suggests the scope of the distortion survey; the distortion survey suggests the location of trial holes; and other clues may have a say, according to their weight. The true cause should be compatible with all the evidence. No potential cause should be abandoned until the evidence disproves it, or at least finds its contribution to be trivial. Once the cause or causes have been established, attention can be focused on severity and prognosis.

If the principle of challenging and eliminating potential causes is followed, even an unintelligent start can be redeemed. Figure 14.14 shows the level survey on a two-storey house. The clear implication appeared to be heave on the corner shown furthest to the right, but investigation at this position found only medium-dense sand, a soil not capable of heave, to a depth of at least 5m. The ground investigation was widened, and found that the house was perched on the edge of a domestic rubbish dump, the highest corner being the only area on natural ground. The nature of the distortion, aided and abetted by the desk study, had been totally misleading. This occasional fate should be welcomed for its educational value.

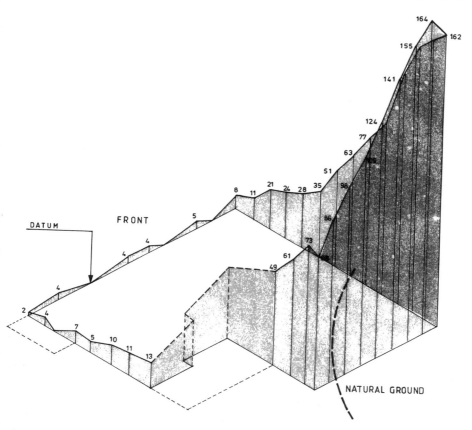

Figure 14.14 *Misleading survey*

Chapter 15

TIMBER FRAME AND
EARTH WALLING

The combination of visual inspection, distortion survey and ground investigation works the same as for masonry, but the practice of it is more difficult. Damage is not as easy to find, let alone interpret. Recent movement may be masked by centuries of distortion. In fact it is not uncommon to find principal members with irrelevant mortices or peg holes which betray the fact that they are secondhand, and part of their distortion may have been earned in a different building.

Neither is it always easy to tell whether the structure is of one material or another. Both internal and external faces of walls may be covered; a brick skin may disguise an original timber frame; and a variety of alterations and extensions may have introduced a mixture of materials.

Age itself is a clue but a frustrating one to pursue without expert help. The evolution of building has not been straightforward. It has had little to do with human skill, which has proved to be the most adaptable resource, but a lot to do with material costs, regional variation, social fashion and even tax laws whose past effects have been as strange as today's.

In the thirteenth century, trees, mud, bricks and stone were all available for building. As we can tell from the survivors, trees gave the best value for money. The early development of timber frame encouraged the development of carpentry and the peak of mutual achievement was reached in the Tudor period.

By late Elizabethan times, timber had to be used more sparingly. At about the same time, the fashion grew for covering the external face instead of infilling with wattle and daub. By the late seventeenth century, there were several options for covering. Render, weatherboarding and tile hanging were the most popular, and the fashion for concealment spread indoors so that there was little of the true structure left on view. Inevitably, standards were relaxed. Carpentry declined. The strength of Tudor timber frame was in its intelligent and skilful joint details, but later buildings began to rely implicity on coverings or infill for stability.

In the seventeenth century, materials other than timber became common. Stone was used increasingly, although high transport costs kept most of it within a small radius of its quarry. New skills were developed for stone quarrying, dressing and laying. As with mediaeval timber, these skills were concentrated on the most important buildings. Areas with no rock outcrops developed skills in small stone such as flint and ironstone boulders, and even in soft rock such as chalk. The use of mud, clay and various mixes of earth, unfired, developed its own particular skills which survived into the nineteenth century.

Meanwhile, brick gradually became a more regular-shaped and easier-to-use material. Its popularity, and its size, waxed and waned with the tax laws but then, within a short period during the mid nineteenth century, the brick tax was abolished, the shape was standardized, mass production was developed and transport became cheaper. From then on, brick was the most popular material. The use of all other materials except, in some areas, stone, declined sharply.

Timber frame inspection

At the planning stage (Chapter 9), the type of timber frame should first be established, before noting any alterations and recording damage.

Timber frame types

Until carpentry declined, timber frame was built as a frame which could stand alone. Bays were erected, typically at 4.5m centres although there was no standard. The bays supported all the floor and roof loads, they restrained the non load bearing infill and their main beams or roof trusses tied the building laterally. Plates and bracing between frames tied the building longitudinally.

Figure 15.1 shows three original types: cruck; post and truss; and aisled. Regional preference was surprisingly rigid. Cruck, for example, was most popular in the north of England and in Wales and was almost unknown in East Anglia. Variations on the main themes are numerous. In East Anglia, for example, it became fashionable to fix posts at close centres (in other words between bays) on external walls. This was known as box framing.

By the seventeenth century, timber building was losing its elegance, mainly because joints were being used for location but not to transfer forces, so that

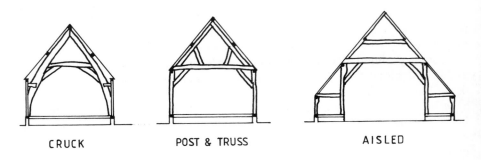

CRUCK   POST & TRUSS   AISLED

Figure 15.1   *Timber-frame types*

frame action was lost and the infill was needed for stability. Infill was sometimes studwork, sometimes brick, sometimes earth or stone. Much of what survives from this *ad hoc* style is ordinary housing which in previous generations hardly outlived its builders, so perhaps it is fairer to describe it as a levelling of standards rather than a decline.

In the nineteenth century, nailed softwood stud walling came into use. This was sometimes storey height (platform frame) and sometimes ran to two storeys (balloon frame). It was the forerunner of modern timber stud, which is known as timber frame although the term is a misnomer since the product acts as a panel, not as a frame.

Alterations

It is necessary to suspend credibility when searching for ill-advised alterations. Statistics can show that every old building must have had at least one lunatic owner, which means that unsafe alteration has been attempted at least once in every mediaeval timber frame. The consequences may in some cases have been immediate, and the rescue urgent. Figure 15.2 shows the case where posts were removed because they were in the way of some furniture. Stability was restored by steelwork.

The most common ill-advised alteration is the cutting of ties to improve headroom or to insert new stairs. The horizontal force previously taken by the tie then gets shared between the external studs and possibly roof members, all doing their best to resist unexpected stretching (Figure 15.3), and all suffering to some extent as a result. Internal partitions were sometimes pierced, in the mistaken belief that they were non load bearing.

Some alterations were made to enlarge the ground floor plan area. In buildings which originally had jetties, the ground-storey external wall was sometimes moved out to be flush with the first storey, seriously increasing stress in the first floor joists. (They not only had further to span, but they lost the benefit of a permanent cantilever tip load.) The H-plan favoured by Tudor

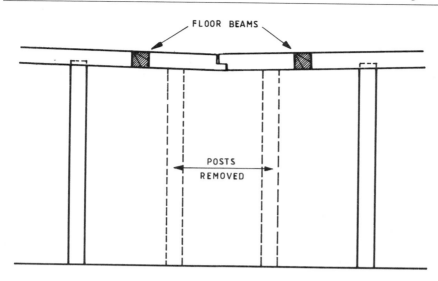

Figure 15.2 *Effect of post removal*

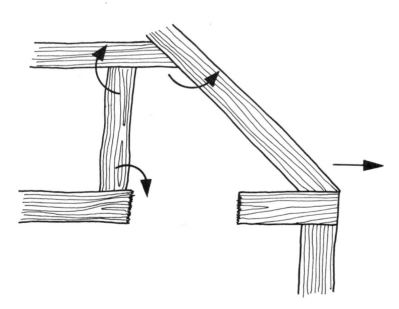

Figure 15.3 *Effect of tie removal*

buildings was sometimes filled in to form a rectangle, and perhaps at a later date one of the principal parts of the H was thoughtlessly shifted.

Windows were enlarged when the tax on them was abolished and larger plate glass became available. This encouraged the cutting of original load bearing mullions. Wattle and daub infill was often replaced by brick which has introduced the long-term problem of rot at the contact between brick and timber.

Some genuine improvements have had relatively minor side-effects. Tannic acid from oak has attacked iron and steel clamps, as well as nails inserted to replace failed dowels in joints. Where less durable softwood has replaced the original hardwood, there has sometimes been a more rapid deterioration, which can usually still be arrested by improving protection from damp.

Damage

True mediaeval timber frame relies on its joints, and these should be inspected for signs of overstress. The most vulnerable are the tension joints (Figure 15.4), whose strength is no more than the wedge or peg which holds them, and the bearing joints (Figure 15.5) which have no resistance to spread. Joints may also fail if subjected to unexpected forces such as racking (Figure 15.6) or bending (Figure 15.7).

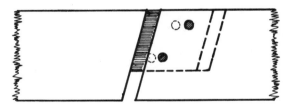

Figure 15.4   *Tension*

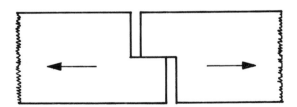

Figure 15.5   *Spread*

It is difficult to tell whether a joint has yielded recently, which would suggest a progressive movement, or has crept through years of moisture content and load changes, which would suggest that there is no serious problem. Recent movement is sometimes advertised by damage to coverings. In Figures 9.5 and 9.6, the external wall damage was noticed by the splitting of decorations.

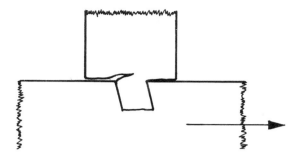

Figure 15.6 *Racking joint*

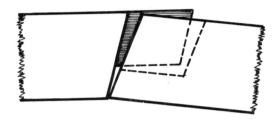

Figure 15.7 *Bending joint*

An old roof is likely to have had more than one covering. Although all types of traditional covering are still in use, thatch and flagstone have lost ground to tiles and slates, so there may be a weight difference between original and present. As a very rough guide, a pitch of 50° or more is typical for a roof which was originally thatched; 45° for plain tiles and flags; 35° for thick slates; 30° for thin slates.

The roof structure itself may not be original. At the very least it is likely to have enjoyed or suffered occasional repair and alteration. Maintenance work was, as a rule, unsophisticated. Old roof trusses are likely to have been patched rather than restored, and unless the patching was unusually efficient a simpler and lower quality construction was attempted. Where old trusses have decayed and reliance is now placed on rafter and ceiling joists, the consequence may be that external walls, previously non-load bearing, now take both a vertical and a horizontal load, with the latter possibly unresolved and the new rafters receiving only limited benefit from the now overspanned purlins.

After an accident, joints should be inspected to see if they have been damaged by out-of-plane forces. After fire they should be inspected for charring, because the timber section is reduced at most joints and the strength of the member will depend on the reduced section, as well as on vulnerable items such as pegs or wedges. The presence of metal within a joint (such as a plate or clamp) increases the likelihood of charring.

When timber building abandoned carpentry, it had to rely on infill or close studding for stability, and the present structural condition of a 'non-frame' timber frame has to be judged in that knowledge. Scarf and lap joints may still have been used, and may still serve a purpose, but it is usually more important to be satisfied that connections between timber and infill are still good. That is generally so with brickwork, provided it has not caused rot, but earth or board infills may have lost some of their value. Distortion may already be evident, as posts and joists respond with less restraint to permanent loading and minor ground movement. Alterations are as much of a menace as with genuine timber frame. Internal walls in particular, which might have been mere partitions within timber frame, often provide essential robustness or even direct support, and any weakening of them can lead to distortion.

Rot and infestation

Detection of rot and infestation was mentioned in Chapter 9. Mediaeval buildings have all the common problems and a few of their own characteristic ones. Some still have their oak sole plates which in most cases need replacing. Damp takes many years to penetrate a substantial hardwood plate, but once there it threatens the studwork with more rapid deterioration because the latter faces the damp end grain-on. The same is true at floor and roof levels. If hardwood plates are the first line of defence they may resist penetration for a long time but, when their defence is breached, will quickly pass on the damp to the studs.

It was mentioned earlier that brick infills can invite damp. So can other types of 'improvement'. In some cases it was thought desirable to fix felt to the roof without going to the trouble of replacing the covering, and this is guaranteed to channel rainwater against timber (Figure 15.8). Interstitial condensation can be introduced to timber studs by insulating wall panels. Roof condensation can be caused by a modest improvement to insulation at ceiling level. Unfortunately, in the UK climate, materials are sensitive to small changes in the environment.

Beetle attack is harder to detect in large timber members. Sometimes a previous damp condition may have encouraged the start of an infestation by death-watch beetle which is still not apparent if the insects have not emerged through the surface being inspected. Whether test cores should be taken would depend on the importance of the survey. If the timber is a principal member which structural appraisal will place reliance on, then it is obviously important to confirm its integrity.

Timber bracing is often cut from thinner wood than posts and beams, and often consists mostly or entirely of sapwood; and furthermore it may be halved across the members it connects. This makes it more than usually vulnerable. Bracing often suffers preferential attack and harbours insects which may eventually spread to other areas.

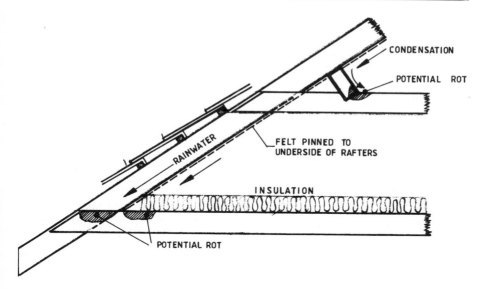

Figure 15.8 *Alteration causing deterioration*

It goes without saying that a building which utterly relies on its timber should, if it is undergoing a comprehensive survey, be thoroughly inspected for rot and infestation.

Distortion survey

Few mediaeval timber frames will not have experienced one or more of the following causes of distortion:

- original shrinkage, often severe because large sections of green timber were used
- gross settlement of the sole plate or stylobates on soft ground, sometimes regenerated by the addition of a brick chimney or other heavy alterations
- timber rot, particularly below ground where it is not noticed
- subsidence, probably inactive, but possibly from more than one incident
- unwise alteration, most commonly causing lateral spread or severe floor deflection
- previous overload, including storm damage
- infestation if severe.

As often as not, a distortion survey hardly seems worthwhile because of the impossibility of untangling the various potential movements. However, if realistic ambitions are set, it can yield surprisingly useful information. For example, where one part of the building is much heavier than the rest, a survey may show distortions to have responded mainly to differential settlement between heavy and light, which would normally be extinct. A suspected local weakness, such as an understrength floor, may be checked for abnormal deflection. Visually apparent leans may raise the question of future stability, and a distortion survey may assist the appraisal in deciding whether improvement has yet become necessary.

Interpretation and appraisal

As for masonry buildings, it is possible to think in terms of the three broad categories: cosmetic damage; serviceability damage; and instability. There is no simple aid to judging the categories, and visual inspection should be supplemented by distortion survey and, if necessary, ground investigation.

Earlier, in the context of foundation settlement, it was suggested that buildings achieve equilibrium after a while even if movement is abnormal. This is true of many timber framed buildings, not just with their foundation settlement but with their sometimes spectacular distortions that evolve over the years. Unless these have reached imminent instability, or are threatened by a recent incident, interpretation and appraisal is concerned mainly with estimating the dangers of decay. Decay is the biggest single threat. Where coverings cannot be removed, advice on decay can only be intelligently speculative.

Earth wall types

Earth walling has distinct regional variations: cob (West Country); clay lump (East Anglia); and wytchert (Buckinghamshire area). There is also a little-used style (Pisé) imported from France.

Cob and clay lump both have clay as the major ingredient, mixed with chalk, sand or grit, the proportions varying between localities. Chopped straw or heather was introduced to prevent the material from becoming too friable on drying out. Enough water was added at the manufacturing stage to allow the mix to be thoroughly consolidated by treading.

In the case of cob, this wet mix was simply moulded into the walls *in situ,* with pauses to allow the material to shrink naturally and gain strength. In the case of clay lump, the mix was formed into standard blocks and used as building blocks, with mud for mortar.

Wytchert is similar to cob, but the mixture contains more chalk than clay. Pisé was a dry-earth process, with no fibre addition, the constituents being rammed into place between shutter boards. In some cases, earth walling was used as an infill in timber buildings.

The properties of earth walling are those of the parent material, modified of course by added soil and fibre, since there was no firing. So there was, and is, a high risk of collapse through saturation, or of shrinkage cracking through desiccation. Buildings of earth were therefore provided with a stone plinth at footing level and a wide overhang at roof level, to avoid saturation at these two critical levels. The buildings, very seldom more than two stories in height, were plain in both plan and elevation, so that there were no ledges to collect rainwater. Walls were regularly lime washed. In exposed places, external coverings such as render (most often), tile hanging or (least often) tar were provided to keep off driving rain.

Earth wall inspection

The thicker (typically 600–1200mm), tapered (often thicker at foot), homely irregularity of cob walls and their rounded corners advertise their origin. Clay-lump walls are thinner (typically 300–500mm), uniform and with straight vertical edges, and are therefore indistinguishable from other plastered and rendered buildings. All earth walling is prone to consolidation under self-weight, and this can sometimes be spotted by the slight downturn of corners of window openings. This is not a frequent occurrence, however, and in any case many windows have been enlarged since consolidation was complete.

Appraisal

Earth walling is weak and readily cracks if it is altered even in a minor way. Figure 15.9 shows the case of an earth wall which bowed and separated from return walls when a lean-to roof, which had previously been restraining it, was removed. Severe wind can more easily knock down earth walling, especially the thinner clay lump which often fractures along a bed course, than any other material.

The greatest threat to earth walling is deterioration. If the weatherproofing is breached, softening and frost damage can cause utter destruction within months. It is therefore important to check that the plinth continues to deter rising damp, that there is protection at eaves level, that no vulnerable spot is left unprotected, and that the external surface is in fine shape. Nowadays, a warmer and drier indoor atmosphere is preferred than previously, and some new shrinkage may have occurred here and there. Such shrinkage must not be allowed to damage the external covering. In the case of wide fractures, any patch repair should use a relatively dry and non-shrinkable material.

Bats

It is an offence (1981 Wildlife and Countryside Act) intentionally to kill or injure bats, damage or destroy their roosts or disturb them while roosting. If

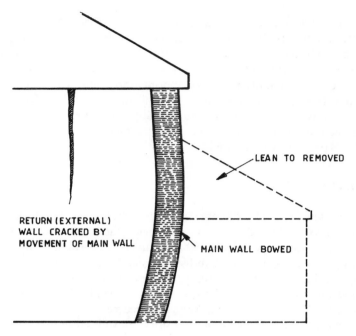

Figure 15.9 *Movement of weak earth wall*

action is proposed which could affect bats or their roosts, the Nature Conservancy Council (local office or Northminster House, Peterborough PE1 1UA) must be informed and given sufficient time to advise on special precautions. Bats hibernate from October to April. The young are born in June or July.

Individual roosts are not always occupied continuously, since bat colonies move seasonally, but the same site tends to be occupied by the same colony at the same season each year. Even if a site is currently occupied, bats are rarely seen during the day. Their roosts may be identified by the presence of droppings which are 4–8mm long, dark brown or black and consist mainly of fragments of insects, easily crumbled. They are usually found under ridge boards, at eaves or close to chimney stacks.

Timber treatment with toxic chemicals must not be carried out, even in the temporary absence of a colony, because the fumes can kill the returning bats. Non-toxic fluids based on synthetic pyrethroids are now widely available, although the Nature Conservancy Council should still be contacted before treatment begins.

Chapter 16

INADEQUATE INFORMATION

If the interpretation fails to home in on a credible cause of damage, the evidence must be inadequate. Either there is too little of it or it carries insufficient weight.

Inadequate information defeats appraisal. In Chapter 13, three possible courses were suggested: widen the scope of investigation; or recommend action which safely circumscribes all the uncertainties; or carry out a more intense study of available information. This chapter considers the third option. It is the least attractive and is not guaranteed to reach a satisfactory conclusion.

In fact it should be prevented from reaching a conclusion as long as it remains inadequate, but the extra work may be good enough to inform a useful tentative opinion. For example, it could be the basis for a period of diagnostic monitoring.

Enhanced evidence

When there is not enough information to apply the compatibility test, some of the lost ground can be made up by intensifying the available evidence. Figure 16.1 shows an 80-year-old office building with rendered external walls, for which an appraisal was required without removing the new decorations. The external survey was therefore of little use, and very little damage was evident internally. However, it was possible to carry out a level survey on the first and second floors at close centres, generally 300mm, except at a few local obstructions. Both surveys had a similar pattern of readings.

By ignoring a few pockets of local variation, a tilt from front to rear could be discerned. This was compatible with extinct differential settlement. The local variations coincided with downpipes, some of which ran internally within brick columns, and these downpipes had been leaking into the sandy sub-soil, causing subsidence. It is possible that a coarser grid of less accurate levels might have missed the local variations which were demonstrating the only active, and therefore the only important, cause of distortion. It is equally possible that thick carpets and cluttered rooms would have defeated the most painstaking level survey. *Ad hoc* inspections make their own luck. Investigation is sometimes restricted to visual inspection and spirit level. This too puts greater pressure on observation and interpretation.

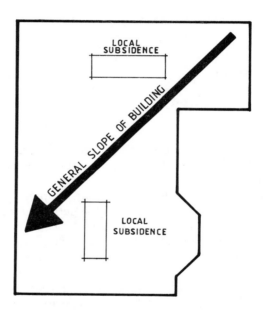

Figure 16.1   *Overall and local distortion.*

Seemingly innocuous features can provide clues. Fillets often disguise separation (Figure 5.4) and distortion (figure 16.2). If an internal door binds, it has either moved on its hinges or its frame has distorted. The latter possibility can be checked by spirit level. Figure 16.3 shows two cases. In (a) the external wall has moved downwards and in (b) it is the floor itself which is deflecting. Further inspection should confirm the pattern and should focus on the detailed cause which might be subsidence in the case of (a) or notched and weakened joists in the case of (b).

Timber frame, at the best of times, challenges the attempt to match damage and distortion. Exposed member connections should display any intolerable movement of the overall building such as longitudinal racking due to

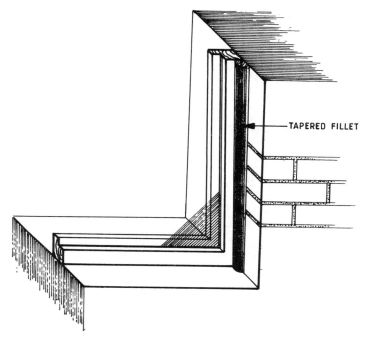

Figure 16.2 *Fillet disguising distortion.*

subsidence or spreading due to horizontal forces. Local problems, such as overloaded beams, will have local effects such as gross deflection or distortion of scarf joints, or in extreme cases splitting and crushing of fibres.

Previous owners, particularly in the case of commercial buildings, may have been more tolerant of damage and careless of maintenance. A history of recent ownership and any work carried out on the building may provide useful clues, but only if there are funds for the time-consuming research.

Most timber frames and coeval buildings are threatened to some degree by deterioration, however gently, and the most successful investigations of all are continuous. If the same person can visit whenever a part is opened up for normal maintenance or redecoration then the succession of inspections will provide an increasingly useful store of knowledge, and will also ensure that decay is dealt with as it is discovered.

The rest of this chapter discusses the interpretation of masonry damage from crack pattern alone, and it carries the disclaimer that in many cases the exercise never rises above the purely speculative.

Limiting tensile strain

Chapter 9 touched on the concept of limiting tensile strain by describing the

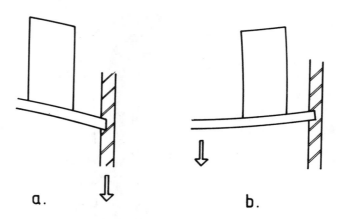

Figure 16.3 *Floor distortions.*

wall as a beam and noting the difference between hogging and sagging (pp. 87–89). The concept was introduced by Burland and Wroth. It has been well described in Building Research Establishment publications, to which reference is recommended for a full understanding. The following is a brief innumerate summary.

Returning to the beam analogy: a masonry wall can be imagined as a beam deflecting under load. Beams have rigid supports, whereas walls on foundations have, at least when first built, continuous support, and their deformation is caused by the settlement of the soil, which is variable even when the conditions are uniform. This does not upset the beam analogy, which says that settlement and strain can be related to the properties and geometry of the wall.

Surveys have found that masonry first cracks at a strain of between 0.05–0.10 per cent. This is its limiting tensile strain. The formulae which connect strain with deflection can therefore be used to define the deflection ratios at which damage can be expected to form.

The concept improved design for settlement of unreinforced masonry because, for the first time, it distinguished between hogging and sagging, and between bending and shear, by producing formulae for different modes of deformation and different properties of walls. Hogging causes cracks to form at the top and propagate downwards; sagging causes cracks to form at the bottom and propagate upwards (Figure 9.3). Hogging causes damage more readily than sagging. It meets less resistance.

In Figure 16.4, damage is caused in diagram (a) by hogging, which only needs to open a few perpend joints and disturb a short length of mortar bed to overcome the resistance of the superstructure. If the wall were topped by a reinforced concrete ring beam (diagram b), then the resistance would be magnified considerably. But the average wall in a traditional building has little effective strength at eaves level. Diagram (c) shows that sagging meets little more resistance than hogging within the wall itself. (In fact, the cracking has for the sake of simple illustration been shown as going through the units as well as the mortar, which would with most masonry increase the overall resistance.) But additional resistance to sagging is provided by the strength of foundations and their friction with the ground. In some cases, the benefit of this resistance is partly lost through slippage along the damp-proof course.

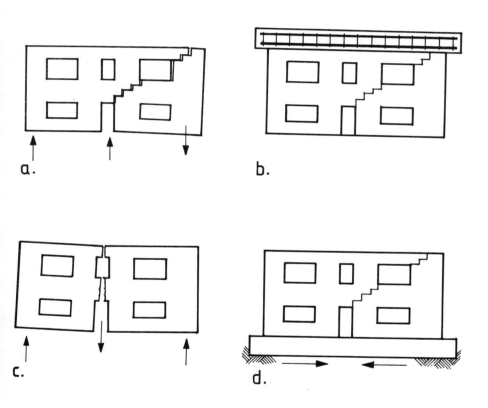

Figure 16.4   *Hogging and sagging*

In Figure 16.4, damage was clearly the result of bending. Often it is not. It can represent shear strain or a combination of bending and shear. The main influence is the shape of the wall. The ratio between 'span' and height (L/H) gets smaller for tall walls. As it does so, bending and shear stiffness both increase, but bending stiffness increases at a faster rate, so shear damage becomes the more likely.

When designing for settlement, then, it is possible to make useful predictions: about the likelihood of bending and shear strain; and about the level at which hogging or sagging deflection might cause damage. When investigating damage, we must start again with the admission that investigation is not the reverse of design, because there are many potential causes for the same damage pattern. At the design stage, for example, the length of wall is obvious. One of the apparent difficulties of investigation is that the 'unsupported' length is unknown (Figure 16.5). In fact, rather than a knife edge between full support and thin air, there is a redistribution of bearing pressure. This cannot be measured. It implies a probably unknown length enduring an unknown reduction in support.

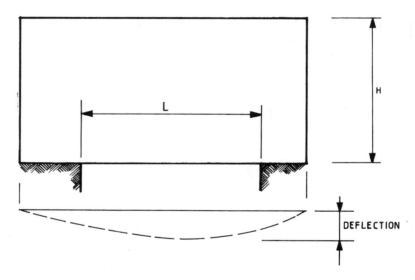

Figure 16.5   *Unsupported length*

But this is not the handicap it first appears to be. The pattern of cracking, principally its taper, should demonstrate whether the mode of deformation is hogging or sagging. If it has no taper, the damage may reflect a shear strain. (If there is differential movement along the line of the crack, between its two faces, shear strain has certainly occurred. That is not always easy to observe.) Thus, it may be possible to work backwards from the visual evidence: judging from its pattern whether the damage is due to bending or shear (assuming it is not a purely superstructure problem such as thermal damage); and judging whether there is hogging or sagging. This should establish the length which has lost support, and that is a useful step in the direction of cause.

The concept also helps to explain the difference in behaviour between original settlement and later subsidence. In Figure 16.6, diagram a shows a long wall which is distorted for its full length, with maximum settlement at mid-point. That is the typical sagging bending mode. Diagram (b) represents distortion caused by subsidence of one end. This would encourage hogging if the wall were to bend. But if only a short length loses support, shear cracking would form in preference to bending because the L/H ratio would be much smaller than in Figure 16.6(a).

In coarse-grained soils, settlement is quick and it occurs as the wall is built. Diagram (c) shows the wall going up, when the L/H ratio is even higher, and in these circumstances a sagging bending response is always the most likely.

Figure 16.6(d) shows that subsidence often begins as a very local loss of support and therefore, during its inception, the L/H ratio is tiny. So early response would be in the form of shear strain. It would be some time before bending were remotely possible. If shear damage occurred first, it would be the focus of further damage, and movement would continue for the time being at that point, even if higher stresses developed elsewhere. Eventually those higher stresses might become intolerable and cause fresh damage. If that situation where to develop, the same cause could display different modes of damage.

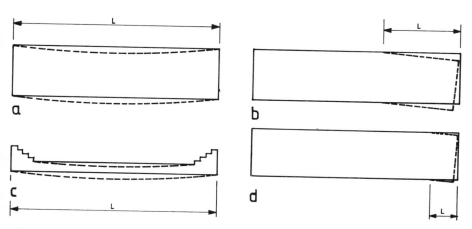

Figure 16.6   *Effect of length to height ratio*

The usual small but unpredictable variations upset the ideal pattern. Variations in wall geometry can transform it. But concept is always valid, as long as the heterogeneous effects on masonry are acknowledged.

Openings and restraints

In a solid wall, shear cracking would be roughly diagonal. Openings locally influence stresses so that even shear cracking might occur in a vertical line.

With regular openings between floor levels, both shear and bending stiffness are reduced, but the flanges of brickwork between heads and cills may be substantial enough to ensure that bending stiffness remains a reasonable proportion of its total wall value. It is not difficult to make at least a qualitative judgement of each case. A two-storey wall with openings immediately below eaves level would in fact have negligible stiffness above first floor level. Another storey would make all the difference, increasing the bending stiffness of the wall as a whole by a factor of probably more than three.

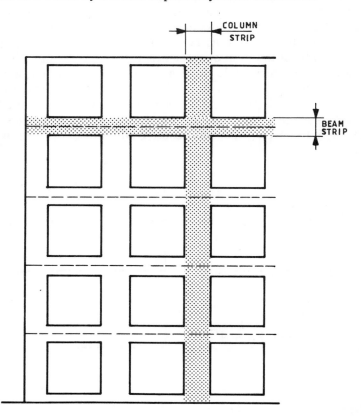

Figure 16.7   *Wall acting as frame*

Tall buildings with large regular openings tend to develop frame action (Figure 16.7) and damage at openings might reflect local panel bending rather than shear. Tall walls with tall openings (Figure 16.8) tend to behave as two linked walls, rather like the bungalow pierced by a door opening, discussed in Chapter 9 (pp. 89). Damage may result from the different behaviour of the two parts. It tends to occur near the openings, with distortion of frames and perhaps even breakage of glass panes. It does not need abnormal foundation movement for its cause, but can occur during normal events such as wind loading, when the two parts respond differently.

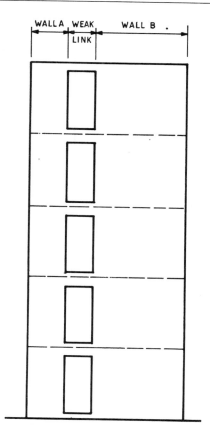

Figure 16.8 *Wall dominated by openings*

Mortar strength

If the strength of mortar is less than the strength of the unit (brick, block or stone), cracking will tend to follow beds and perpends: otherwise it will affect the units themselves. Poor adhesion between unit and mortar, sometimes the result of frost action during construction or the use of high-suction bricks, can encourage mortar-only cracking as the tenuous bond is ruptured. It can lead to a form of punching shear, as an unsupported panel simply falls away, leaving corbelled masonry above it.

Damage related to movement

A judgement on mode of cracking is one step towards its cause. The next step is to imagine the movement behind it. A variety of crack types can be envisaged, each determined by the properties of the materials, the geometry

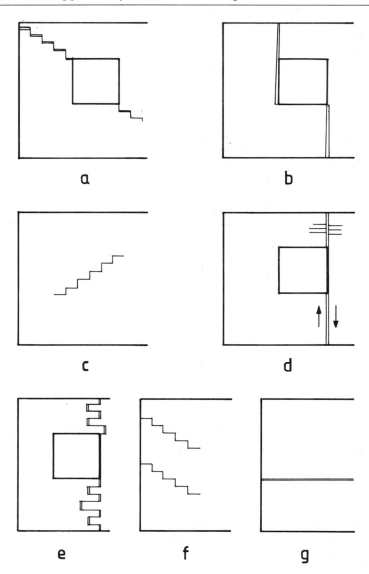

Figure 16.9   *Crack patterns*

of the wall, its restraints, and of course the movement causing the damage. Figure 16.9 shows a sample. Tapered mortar cracking, typical of bending, is shown at (a). Where the mortar is strong and the unit weak, a more vertical line might be followed, as at (b), where an upward tapering crack signifies sagging. At (c) diagonal shear cracking is shown. Vertical shearing is shown at (d). At (e) there is pure elongation. Torsional cracking, which might be

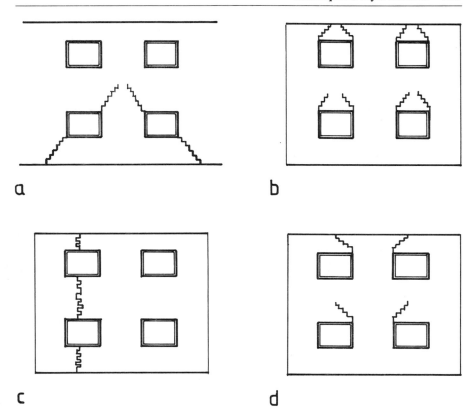

Figure 16.10 *Damage attracted to openings*

caused by a horizontal twist during wind loading or remote subsidence, is shown at (f). At (g) there is out-of-plane bending caused by the building tilting away from the observer.

Figure 16.10 shows some of the possible types of cracking at windows. At (a) the cracks are wider at the bottom, suggesting that there is sagging bending and therefore a loss of support between the cracks. The example at (b) also implies a downward rotation between cracks, but this time suspicion centres on the lintels, or their absence. Example (c) has no taper and no vertical displacement. These features should be confirmed by close inspection, and a note made of any nearby restraints which may be dominating behaviour, but when a crack steps to and fro instead of following a vertical or diagonal line, purely horizontal movement is a strong probability.

In examples (a) and (b) the movement can be crudely imagined as wedges of masonry moving downwards and away from the line of the cracks. The pattern shown in example (d) is more difficult to understand. It is unlikely to represent lintel deflection because that would normally cause equal rotation

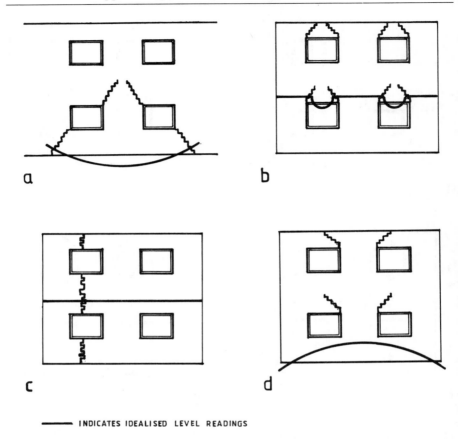

a

b

c

d

INDICATES IDEALISED LEVEL READINGS

Figure 16.11   *Damage explained by level survey*

at either bearing. The pier between windows cannot be moving down. The pattern defies that possibility. If the central pier is moving up, then the pattern is credible. In shrinkable clay areas, such a pattern is not uncommon, and heave is the frequent cause. Cracks are not always tapered because the mode of damage may be punching shear. However, this demonstrates the limitations of diagnosis from a visual inspection alone. Other interpretations are possible. For example, the pier might be stable, with the wall on either side settling. We might say that was less likely because cracking should have developed at the opposite corners of the openings rather than, with suspicious symmetry, right next to the pier, but another piece of evidence would be needed for proof.

Figure 16.11 shows the same crack patterns with the level surveys superimposed. Doubts are resolved. The examples are, of course, glib. In real cases, both crack pattern and level survey would be disturbed by the inherent material and dimensional variations, but that does not detract from the obvious improvement gained by combining the two sources of evidence.

This returns us to the original point about inadequate information. It can be supplemented by enhanced evidence or enhanced interpretation, which can both be useful as long as the boundaries of conjecture are respected.

Chapter 17

SUDDEN DAMAGE

Catastrophic failure is the result of either an irresistible load, which even the best-constructed building would fail to withstand, or normal loading on a sensitive structure. These two groups are discussed in turn.

Overload: vehicular impact

Impact has to be absorbed by the building. If the vehicle strikes a weak wall, say an infill between timber frames, it will cause very severe but local damage. It may, if there has been little to check its momentum, continue to penetrate the building, and incidents do occur where vehicles pass right through one building and enter another. Well-built buildings, with all parts tied together, are better able to reduce momentum and absorb the shock because their entire weight is mobilized as soon as the vehicle strikes. The force is thereby spread over a larger area and although damage is less serious than with a weak building it can often be more widespread. Timber connections, straps and ties some distance from the impact may suffer damage serious enough to need repair.

Timber frame buildings have a lower mass than masonry and may therefore receive a larger shock. However, they often absorb this shock better than masonry because their tensile strength and impressive stiffness under short-term loading gives them greater resilience. Sometimes the bounce of a timber frame building is demonstrated by the small permanent displacement of fittings, such as worktops, which do not return to their original positions. A fair amount of bounce can be tolerated without permanent damage. Damage is most serious when an external corner of the building is hit, and worst of all when the corner was relying on a single column or timber post for support.

The most frequent causes of a vehicle losing control are driver unfitness, driver evasion and weather conditions. Road geometry can multiply the risk. Typical hazards are bends, especially when the change of direction is vertical as well as horizontal, and unexpected narrowing, particularly at edges of built-up areas. If a hazard coincides with a frost pocket, as may occur with a change of direction at the bottom of a dip, then the danger is greater still.

Vehicles very rarely deviate by more than 45° from their previous direction, and usually they deviate by much less. The most severe damage occurs within three metres of the road edge, although buildings at the bottom of unobstructed slopes beyond the road could of course still be within range.

Vehicles and buildings will never be segregated, so a residual risk has to be accepted. Protection should be considered where the hazard is exceptional, or the building is vulnerable because of its construction, and where the potential loss of life is serious because of the building's function. Protection usually requires planning permission. Crash barrers are simplest; width and height restrictions, if physically enforced, the most effective.

Overload: blast

Gas explosions can originate from a number of possible incidents. Unfortunately, some people still keep cylinders indoors and leakage can occur at faulty valves and worn hoses. Leakage from mains can occur when pipes are fractured by subsidence, or traffic vibration, or frost, or simply by slow ground strains. Corrosion, or unfortunate details such has hard spots crossing the path of the pipe and causing differential subsidence, add to the risk. Migration of landfill gas, within the ground and into the building through its unsealed ground floor, is a rare but not unknown event.

The next requirement for an explosion is that the gas should build up indoors to a critical proportion of the atmosphere without being detected. Buildings with ducts and uninhabited basements provide this opportunity. When gas reaches danger proportions inside habitable areas it usually does so during the occupants' absence.

A trivial incident can then cause the actual explosion. Pressure builds up within microseconds and can theoretically, if the mixture is 'ideal', reach the devastating level of $700 kN/m^2$, but it is always reduced by venting. Typical maximum pressures within buildings are in the range of $20–30 kN/m^2$.

The degree to which venting can reduce the maximum pressure depends on the size of the vent, compared with the overall area of wall or floor, and its strength. Glass windows are weak, but their weakness is not predictable. The pressure at which they blow out can vary within wide limits even for single glazing but they are nevertheless the first things to go. Doors blow out at high pressure, causing impact damage to whatever surface they meet afterwards. Non load bearing partitions are the next to go.

The general formula for maximum blast pressure is $AP + BK$. A and B are constants which depend on the fundamental burning velocity of the gas mixture. P is the pressure at which the venting element breaks. Single glazing breaks typically at 7–14 kN/m². K is the smallest cross-sectional area of the room divided by the vent area.

Since practically nothing stands up to the theoretical maximum pressure, the explosion will almost instantaneously create some venting in its immediate vicinity, and this will determine the pressure at which the gas then expands in all directions. It will move through and out of the building, taking the line of least resistance. Further venting may occur. Other materials in its path, including structural members, may fail without venting. In other words, they will be fractured and displaced but not removed. Failure pressures are between 100–200 per cent of static capacity. Figure 17.1 illustrates a gas explosion which destroyed the lightweight single storey extension where the incident occurred, and then entered the two storey area, where it was deflected up the stairwell after causing yield-line fractures to the load bearing stairwell partition. It left the building at eaves level, causing ceiling damage and displacement of struts supporting part of the roof.

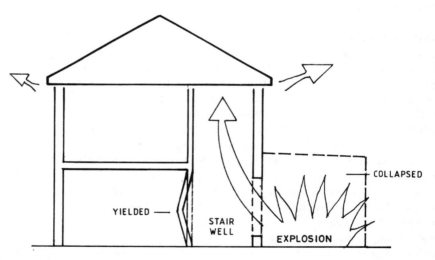

Figure 17.1   *Path of explosion*

The displacement of simple struts, which were not tied at either end, is a small example of the weakness of traditional buildings in the face of explosions. In normal circumstances traditional buildings are stabilized by gravity. A brick wall, for example, resists wind pressure all the better if it is loaded as well as restrained at panel edges. In fact, the tendency to flex during wind gusting will often increase vertical compressive stress (as the top of the wall rotates and attempts to lift whatever is above it), and this action supplies the wall with a gratuitous safety factor. An explosion, however, removes vertical load at the same time as it applies horizontal pressure (Figure 17.2), so that the wall's resistance must rely almost entirely on its bending tensile capacity, which is weak and unpredictable, especially along horizontal bed courses.

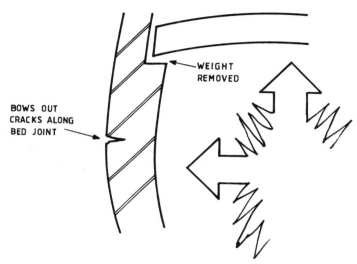

Figure 17.2 *Damage caused by explosion*

Framed buildings are less likely to be destroyed. The frame itself usually survives and goes on supporting whatever is left of the floors and walls when the explosion departs. Timber frame with weak infill may survive almost unscathed, while losing large areas of partition, but where external masonry has been substituted and well tied to the frame, the maximum blast pressure will be higher and the frame at greater risk. Unframed timber building is less resistant.

As with impact, the source of the hazard has an influence on severity. Corners are again the most vulnerable areas. If the blast removes the corner column or the two load bearing walls which meet at the corner, then the structure above is called upon, in its probably weakened condition, to cantilever over whatever gap has formed.

Very often the extent of collapse depends on the building's ability to form corbels, arches or catenaries across missing supports. Masonry is good at arching, but if a corner disappears the best it can do is to corbel. Floors are often able to act in catenary for short periods because of the tensile strength of their boarding. Explosion is often followed by conflagration, so that the building suffers from two separate sources of damage.

Inspecting sudden damage

After severe impact or blast damage, the investigator has to make both an urgent and a long-term appraisal. Stability is the immediate concern and there is no time to carry out more than a visual inspection. Walls left leaning and unrestrained may need shoring or demolishing. In extreme cases, there is no safe alternative to clearing the area and waiting for collapse. Facades left standing and unconnected, or at least not usefully connected to cross walls and floors, are in danger of collapsing soon afterwards during modest wind forces, even if they are more or less vertical, and they should be shored to give positive (in other words held and not merely propped) lateral support at centres of not more than 30 times their thickness. Spacing should be closer if the wall is handicapped by any weakness such as: bulging; eccentric loadings; large openings (shoring either side of every opening may then be necessary); or separation between inner and outer leaves.

Chimney stacks are often left behind after floors and roofs have disappeared. They are not strong elements if they are pierced at floor levels for hearths, and little reliance should be placed on any dividing walls within them. If they have rocked on a bed course during the incident, they will have no reserve tensile strength.

Any small pier of masonry or isolated timber post needs inspecting. If there has been any loss of restraint (or in the case of timber any failure of joints), shoring should be supplied at or near head level to prevent movement in any direction. Arches will be dangerously weakened if damage crosses their line of thrust or removes too much of any counterweight above their springing (Figure 17.3).

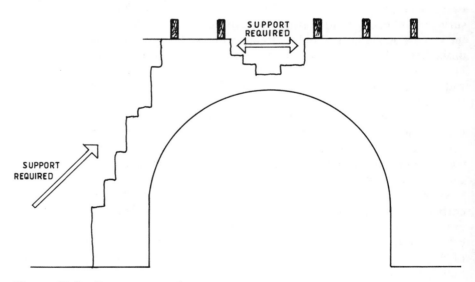

Figure 17.3   *Damage to arch*

After the incident, a floor may be supporting several times its normal load in the form of collapsed debris, and it may itself have been weakened to the point where it is relying on its boarding to act in catenary over part of the area. If it is unsafe, a decision has to be made whether to prop or demolish (or again to clear the area if collapse is imminent). Its removal may introduce another problem. It may reduce the stability of a supporting wall; on the other hand, if the floor has been badly twisted or is partly hanging from the wall its removal may be a relief from dangerous new stresses.

When the building has been made safe, it should be secured as far as possible against vandals, adventurers and the weather. It is often a long time before permanent repairs can be started, and an open building deteriorates very quickly.

Long-term appraisal can be based on the same techniques of inspection as for safe buildings: visual inspection, distortion survey and testing where necessary. Cracked mortar can usually be fully restored by deep pointing, but that is usually the least of the structural problems. Detailed observation is necessary to ensure that all structural damage and distortion is recorded and appraised. Shock may have weakened masonry joints (particularly bed courses) and timber-frame joints; distortions may have introduced more onerous requirements for ties and straps. Walls can be evaluated according to the strength of their individual units (brick, block or stone), with any allowance for weakening in the case of fire, and for the strength reducers discussed in Chapter 3 (pp.17–20). Walls which are in two leaves, whether or not they have a cavity between them, should be inspected for possible loss of integrity between the leaves.

In the case of timber members, their faults are mainly self evident. If timber members survive short-term overloading without damage to their fibres, they will be suitable for re-use. If there are signs of deterioration not related to the sudden damage, such as rusting wall ties or local rot, it will be more economic in the long term to see to them at the same time than to wait until attention becomes essential some months or years after the building has been repaired.

Fire

There is no standard description of fire growth because at every stage it is sensitive to small changes in temperature, air supply, fuel, waste gases and other factors. The following outline covers the typical stages of a straightforward fire.

Ignition leads to smouldering or small flames, at first confined to the immediate locality or room. The early growth of the fire depends at first on the availability of fuel in close proximity, but if this is ample enough to give it a good start ventilation soon becomes as important. In a small enclosed area with doors and windows shut the fire may die out when the oxygen has been used up. It may of course die back to the smouldering stage, only to flare up if fresh oxygen is supplied. A shattered window would serve this purpose very well.

With adequate oxygen, burning of ignitable material will continue. Hot gases will quickly rise to the level of the ceiling which will first act as a barrier, causing horizontal spread of flames and radiating heat downwards at long range from the original ignition. This encourages the fire spread. With continuing fire growth, the layer of hot gases will reach temperatures of 500°C or more and will thicken.

Lining materials which are flammable provide extra fuel. Lining materials which are non-flammable inhibit growth which can then only continue as long as there is fuel in the form of furniture or stored materials. Lining materials which are non-flammable but good insulators will radiate the heat, encouraging the spread of fire within the compartment; long flames may develop.

Flashover is the moment when there is a sudden acceleration in the growth of the fire, after which it becomes very difficult to control. There is no exact definition of flashover, but it is typically accompanied by a rapid rise in temperature and the production of toxic gases, carbon monoxide usually being the most important. Unburnt gases within the hot layer may ignite spontaneously. Flames will probably emerge from the building.

From then on the fire is controlled by ventilation. Hot gases will issue from the building and will very quickly spread within it if dividing walls and ceilings fail. Openings in external walls will provide an excellent air supply, especially if this is wind assisted or drawn in to replace the emerging gases.

Fire starts to decay if the fuel supply runs down, if ventilation is frustrated or if the supply of air is cool enough to sufficiently reduce flame and surface temperatures. If the fire is fought without difficulty of access or equipment or water, the control time is roughly related to the square root of the area of the fire. After fire fighting the building is usually left saturated and undergoing varying rates of cooling.

The fibre structure of timber is not destroyed by heat alone, and what remains beneath the charring line is as good as new. With mediaeval timber, connections will suffer disproportionate damage if member thickness is reduced to form them (Figure 17.4); also, individual pegs may lose strength. Modern bolts, plates and metal connectors are also weakened.

Often the greatest danger to timber is the long-term effect of the water used for fire-fighting purposes. This may lead to rot, even dry rot if the moisture content lingers in the danger zone (20–40 per cent) for long enough. If the building contains important non-structural timber such as panelling, this will need expert attention (often material can be removed and restored off site) but as far as the structural timber is concerned the kindest treatment is to make the building weatherproof and dry as quickly as possible, using heaters and de-humidifiers in combination where necessary.

Most other materials are permanently weakened to a degree which depends on the temperature and duration of the fire in their vicinity. Any colour change in plain concrete signifies a loss of strength. Colour change starts at around 300°C. For a more accurate assessment, laboratory tests can be carried out on

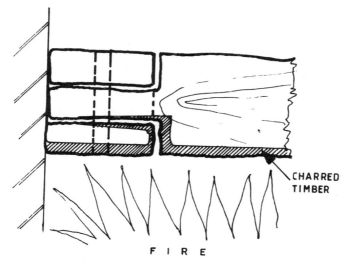

Figure 17.4 *Timber connection charred*

small specimens to establish the thermal exposure and thereby the residual strength of the concrete. Any material can be tested directly for its strength by cutting out cores or units for crushing. There may have been large variations of fire intensity, and the worst conditions should of course be sought for each material.

Bricks are fired materials, and suffer modest re-firing without damage. Signs of surface spalling or fusing indicate high temperatures and at least a degree of weakening, which may be only local. As a rough guide, clay brickwork is unlikely to lose more than 25 per cent of its compressive strength, or calcium silicate more than 50 per cent. Tensile strength and stiffness may be lost to a greater degree. These rely more on the mortar, which should be examined closely. It will have suffered more than the bricks, but repointing will restore it adequately in most cases. Since brickwork is seldom stressed to its limits, the loss of strength it suffers by fire is rarely critical.

Stonework is, even more commonly than brickwork, working at very low stress, and its loss of strength too is often unimportant. Nevertheless, it can suffer a greater degree of weakening than brickwork. Some stones change colour like concrete, but too unpredictably to be relied upon as even an initial guide, so if there is evidence that the fire was intense, even locally, some formal assessment is advisable.

More often than not, with traditional buildings, it is the accompanying damage, in the form of distortions and cracking, which needs remedial attention rather than the material loss of strength. This requires observation on the lines discussed earlier in this chapter (pp.169–71).

Apart from direct destruction, fire causes expansion. The top of the building may tend to elongate and move outwards, causing tensile stresses which sometimes damage timber frame joints and often cause horizontal cracking in masonry. Figure 17.5 shows a case of expansion damage which was severe because the building, although tall, was single storey so that the roof heated up quickly. As this consisted of purlins supported on steel trusses, expansion was quick and large, and the masonry offered little resistance. The roof returned to normal size on cooling, leaving unacceptable permanent distortions.

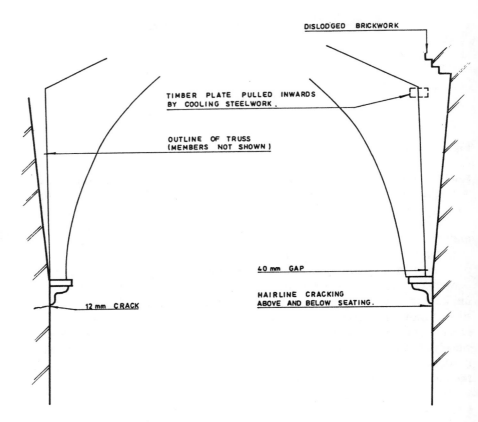

DISLODGED BRICKWORK

TIMBER PLATE PULLED INWARDS
BY COOLING STEELWORK.

OUTLINE OF TRUSS
(MEMBERS NOT SHOWN)

40 mm GAP

HAIRLINE CRACKING
ABOVE AND BELOW SEATING.

12 mm CRACK

Figure 17.5   *Expansion damage*

Slope instability

Slope instability can be sudden and irresistible, although that is not inevitable. It can instead be in the form of recurrent large ground strains, in which case any building in its path acts as a retaining wall, inadequately so unless specifically designed. The cause of damage is, in the latter case, not always obvious. It has to be sought by recording the pattern of damage and distortion, and checking whether they are compatible with pressure applied below ground level and parallel to the slope. There may be a history of previous damage, and there may be clues from the surface of the ground itself.

Unless the instability has been created by man, for example by steepening an already marginally stable hillside, there will very often be signs of previous movement in the vicinity (Figure 17.6). Trees which lean downhill at the base of their trunks may have experienced downslope movement early in their life; a backward lean may be recording an old rotational slip. Rotational slips also cause irregular surface features, especially at the toe of the slope, which may seem crumpled compared with the land immediately beyond.

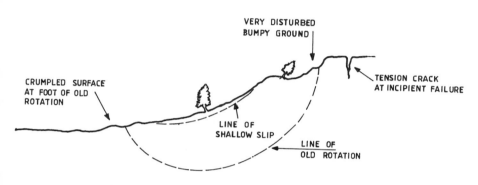

Figure 17.6 *Signs of slippage*

When the unstable ground is a relatively thin sheet of weak material, there may be signs of it having piled up over the years behind the building or any other substantial obstruction.

These clues to instability may be spotted before damage is done. In addition, incipient movement may be heralded by tension cracks uphill of the unstable ground. But surface inspection, before or after the event, can only give lightweight clues. Accurate assessment of land instability requires geotechnical expertise which few general practitioners, architects, surveyors or engineers, possess. The cost of the necessary ground exploration, testing and analysis will usually overshadow the cost of the structural inspection itself.

Rock faces may, as normal weathering takes its toll, shed blocks or boulders onto a building with fatal consequences. They may also contribute to a steep reservoir of scree ready to slip downhill. It is possible to stabilize rock faces or collect or deflect debris, but again the work requires specialist experience and is always costly.

Man-made scree, in the form of colliery tips, spoil heaps and tailings, is stable only at shallow slopes because it is loose and quickly formed, compared with its natural counterparts, and is therefore weak and badly drained. Most is now under control. If there are doubts about any man-made slope, the owners should be informed and there should not be any cases where they can neither demonstrate nor investigate stability.

Excavation can create slope instability. In the case of a clay slope, trenching at either the top or the toe shortens the length of the slip circle (Figure 17.7). As this is the line along which the soil mobilizes its resistance to movement, and as the margin of safety is often not large even with inherently stable slopes, this action can very easily lead to instability. It need not occur immediately. The land may remain marginally stable until a small change in soil properties triggers off the movement, and that could happen some time later, even after the trench or trenches have been back-filled.

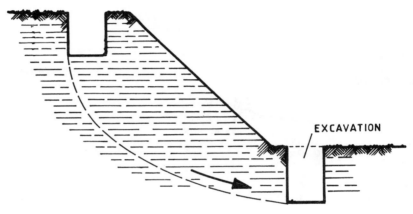

Figure 17.7   *Instability: fine soil*

Slopes which are not predominantly clay may still be close to instability, if the gradient is near the angle of repose of the material, especially if there is seepage or a high ground water level. This type of slope can also collapse as a result of quite modest excavation (Figure 17.8). Usually it happens quickly.

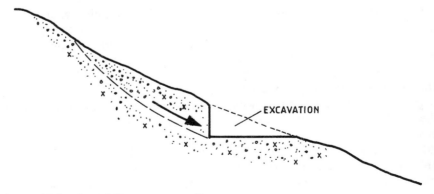

Figure 17.8   *Instability: coarse soil*

It is seldom obvious that a slope is likely to be made unstable by excavation. Casual appraisal is dangerous because factors which determine future behaviour can only be discerned by ground investigation and can only be interpreted by engineers with geotechnical expertise. You can sometimes get away with the wrong diagnosis on a building, but not with a slope.

Trenches and excavation

Simple excavation on land alongside a building is often made without consideration because it is not universally understood that foundations need lateral as well as vertical support (Figure 17.9). In the absence of information on the building or soil, no excavation should be started unless it is at least four times as far from the building as its intended depth. Of course, good foundations, favourable soil conditions or well-controlled and supported excavations would allow this rule of thumb to be relaxed, but even a safe excavation should not be left to deteriorate. It has been known for inexperienced underpinners to dig down to foundation level along an entire wall as stage one of the operation, and on more than one occasion this has resulted in the building's collapse.

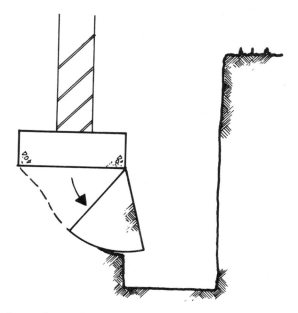

Figure 17.9 *Lateral instability*

Any unsupported excavation yields laterally, and so does the soil behind it. A wall founded within this yielding zone, although it need not necessarily collapse in the manner shown in Figure 17.9, may nevertheless experience the ground strains which operate perpendicular to the trench line (Figure 17.10). The wall, assuming it is more or less parallel to the trench sides, has very little strength or stiffness in the direction of the applied force, and it may suffer serious out-of-plane damage. As with so many ground movements, the actual onset of movement and damage can be delayed, especially if the soil has a high clay content. This delay can generate a false sense of security.

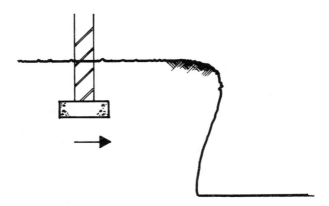

Figure 17.10   *Lateral strain*

It is customary, when planning deep excavations in built-up areas, to assess the potential movement, to devise methods of reducing it where necessary and to monitor both the ground and the nearby buildings so as to confirm the design and control progress.

Other causes

Almost any common cause of damage can occasionally have an extreme effect. In the case of rot, a house with floor joists built into a wet wall is hardly likely to suffer the consequences suddenly because one or two joist ends will fail first and betray the cause by local damage. However, where a building relies for the support of a substantial part of its floor area on a single timber beam, one end of which is vulnerable and inaccessible, there is more of a potential for disaster.

Very exceptional wind loading can of course overcome even well-built buildings. Walls whose restraints are far apart and not rigid are at greatest risk. So are buildings with projections or large openings (Figure 17.11). In fact large openings, such as doors for commercial vehicles, should be closed during storms, so as to reduce wind pressure.

Alterations can cause sudden damage. When this occurs, it needs to be established whether the damage resulted from a weakening of the structure or

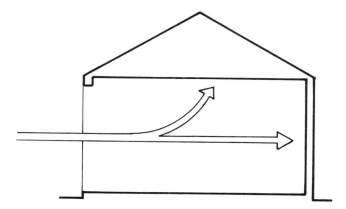

Figure 17.11 *Wind and large opening*

from the method of working. Figure 17.12 shows the case of a frame inserted to replace a load-bearing wall. Severe distortion attended the removal of temporary supports after the frame had been inserted. The frame, however, remained plane and the cause was found to be a failure to properly connect the altered building to the new frame.

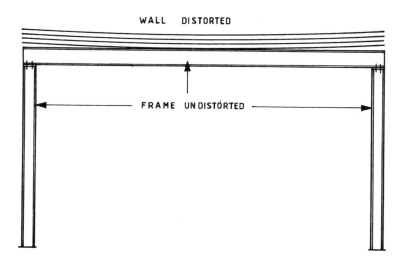

Figure 17.12 *Badly executed alteration*

Demolition is the ultimate alteration, and it has a poor record of unplanned collapses because the work is often done hastily and without supervision. Debris is sometimes allowed to build up and overload floors and their supports.

Sensitivity

A building is sensitive if small changes cause sudden and severe damage, and this most often occurs when it contains large poorly restrained elements.

Modern trussed rafters have tiny longitudinal stiffness. Their manufacturers emphasize the need for bracing in the plane of the rafters, the ceiling joists and the inclined struts.

Adopting manufacturers' recommendations should assure stability. On domestic buildings, it is often possible to get away with not doing so because longitudinal forces are small enough to be resisted by ceiling boards and battens, although they are not intended for that purpose and what little restraint that they provide at the start can disappear during moderate loading such as wind. Above a certain roof size the bracing becomes essential; its omission dangerous. It is difficult to say what this limiting size is, but buildings with 10m roof spans have suffered severe damage from trivial incidents.

Without diagonal bracing, a large roof fails to control creep and other longitudinal forces due to drying shrinkage and differential temperature expansion. If the roof lengthens, it presses against one or both gables which may fail as cantilevers along the eaves-level bed joint.

A number of other faults can make a roof sensitive. If the trusses are fixed out of plumb, ordinary vertical loads will incur longitudinal forces, although a well-braced roof, even a large one, will usually cope. A potentially more serious erection fault is damage during storage or lifting, causing for example the gang-nail connections to loosen and lose their strength and stiffness.

Not all damage to large roofs is critical. Even well-fixed trussed-rafter roofs can, if large, undergo considerable node deflections and damage ceiling boards or partitions, but the problem usually remains cosmetic.

Figure 17.13 shows the plan of an L-shaped building which was not provided with rafter bracing. The wider stem of the L was 11m. Around most of the perimeter, rafters were joined by tiling battens which provided restraint, albeit less than advisable restraint. In the shaded areas, battens were omitted because the rafters did not directly support the roof covering. A slight overload at ceiling level (from water tanks) was sufficient to cause the rafters to bow 50mm out of plane before buckling.

When floors are overloaded there is usually ample warning. Floor collapse is more often associated with a sudden loss of bearing after horizontal movement (Figure 14.12). The horizontal movement can arise for a number of reasons: creep, either singular or cyclic; foundation movement causing supports to rotate and move horizontally away from the beam or joist; weakening of ties in timber frame buildings.

Churches which rely on aisles or buttresses to withstand horizontal forces at roof level can suffer severe damage if these supports are removed or decay. An arch roof will increase its horizontal thrust if the crown is damaged. If the problem were allowed to develop to the point of collapse it is the outward buckling of one or both walls which is likely to be the final event.

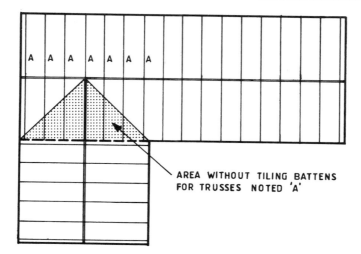

AREA WITHOUT TILING BATTENS
FOR TRUSSES NOTED 'A'

Figure 17.13   *Unrestrained rafter instability*

Tall walls made thick to reduce their slenderness are heavy, and if they have shallow foundations the bearing pressure may be closer to ultimate (failure value) of the soil than is normally the case with traditional buildings. Foundations may then be vulnerable to two types of seemingly small changes. First, loss of ground support, such as by trenching (Figure 17.9) would be more immediately disastrous than with lighter buildings. Even a slight lowering of the ground level, perhaps carried out to reduce damp penetration, could be sufficient to allow lateral failure.

The other problem is sensitivity to ground creep, whether long term or seasonal. Either shrinkage or softening is likely to occur regularly near the surface of clays or silts, and if heavy foundations are very shallow they are liable to bed down due to overload. As the shrinkage or softening is greater on the outside face of the building, the inside having some protection from seasonal changes, tilt may develop over the years which is not well resisted because the wall lacks horizontal restraint. This tilt may then be mistaken for roof spread. It may take a distortion survey and ground investigation to distinguish between the alternative causes.

Gables in Victorian buildings are sometimes only half a brick thick above eaves level, making them particularly vulnerable to roof creep and wind suction. In fact, gables are often thin or of inferior brickwork for their full height, probably because they were not built to carry loads. Unfortunately, most old walls only enjoy horizontal restraint from the floors they support, not from floors which run parallel to them. If a gable supports no floors or roof members, it may have little or no restraint at these levels and may therefore be all the more vulnerable to long-term creep.

The weak gable typifies the problem of appraising old buildings. Whereas the building as a whole is likely to be at peace with its environment, having survived early settlement, it may have some sensitive details which could allow unexpected damage. Fortunately, many cases of sensitivity, as long as they are identified, can be improved simply and at modest cost.

Chapter 18

MONITORING

Any type of movement can be monitored. Two requirements must be fulfilled: the method must be capable of detecting movement below the threshold of damage; and the results must be unambiguous.

Electronic equipment can measure settlement, tilt or vibration of buildings or soils, and it can be especially useful in urban redevelopment, where new work has to be executed without threatening the safety or serviceability of its established neighbours. Permanent insertion of electronic monitoring can provide either an early warning of movement or a long-term record, with obvious benefits to both safety and economy.

But most opportunities for monitoring concern mundane buildings with simple problems, and relatively unsophisticated methods are the most appropriate. The most common form of monitoring, and the simplest, is crack width measurement. Readings can be taken at regular intervals by, in ascending order of accuracy: overlapping plastic tell-tales; screws measured by calipers; and dots measured by demec gauge (Figure 18.1).

Tell-tales record horizontal and vertical movement, but the other two methods require three reference points to form a right angle so that the true direction and magnitude of crack movement can be measured. The legs of the right angle need not be horizontal and vertical, although that normally coincides with the most convenient resolution of strain. The demec gauge, which is preferred on grounds of accuracy, will detect every moisture and thermal perturbation, and these have to be allowed for when interpreting the results.

The main disadvantage of crack monitoring is that it merely watches the symptoms. Results can be ambiguous. A crack may form for one reason and progress for another. Previous load eccentricity or foundation movement, for

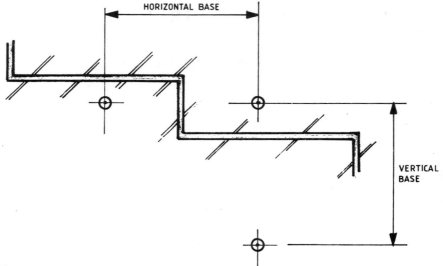

Figure 18.1   *Crack montoring*

example, might have been causing stress without damage. This would start to work its way out as soon as a crack formed for whatever reason, and it might take a little while to do so as the forces are redistributed through the building. All this activity would register without clear meaning on the crack monitoring.

There are two other ways in which accuracy might be compromised. Fresh cracking may develop. If it is not measured, there would be an underestimate of activity. Second, cyclic or seasonal movement may not register equally during the closing phase; effects which in theory should be entirely reversible may prove to be mildly progressive. Figure 18.2 shows a block of flats which cracked at the two stairwells as a result of early foundation movement. The cracks grew. This could have been a symptom of continuing movement, but other causes were equally plausible, and remedial action had to be delayed until the scope of monitoring was widened.

Monitoring has to obey the same rules as investigation. It has to provide enough evidence, using more than one viewpoint if necessary, to isolate the true cause. If the problem concerns foundation movement, then direct monitoring of foundations has an obvious advantage: it gets much closer to the cause. At its simplest, foundation monitoring consists of taking readings by a surveyor's level on a number of stations at the perimeter of the building. This should detect differential movement of 1mm or more.

If absolute movement is required, and this is much preferred, a reliable datum must be installed. In natural granular soil, any rod well driven into undisturbed soil will serve, provided it can be protected from damage during use. Unstable soil obviously has to be penetrated and isolated from the datum (Figure 18.3). If ground-water levels or pore pressures are required, a deep datum can also be made to serve as a piezometer, although it will only serve

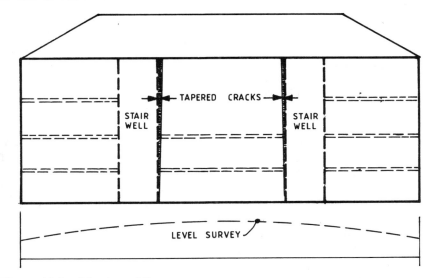

Figure 18.2 *Monitored flats*

as a single point reading, and pore pressure may be needed at a number of levels.

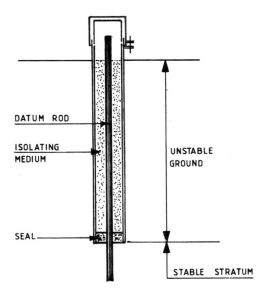

Figure 18.3 *Deep datum*

If it is worth going to the trouble of setting up deep datum monitoring, then it is worth having a large number of stations so that differential movement over short distances can be observed. In areas where the public has easy access, stations should either be protected or placed out of accident range. They can be of the screw-in type which are taken away after readings. It has been found, however, that galvanized nails protruding no more than 25mm from the face of the building are not particularly vulnerable and certainly no target for vandals, and these are suitable for domestic or commercial buildings with minimal public access. One house, returned to after 12 years, had lost only one of its 12 nails.

Crack width and deep datum monitoring make a useful combination, capable of providing adequate information on most straightforward cases of foundation movement. The case shown in Figure 18.2 was resolved when deep datum monitoring was started as a supplement to crack width monitoring, and proved that foundation movement was insignificant. Shrinkage of precast floors was the cause of cracks growing. This was not a long-term problem, and remedial works were able to be confined to the insertion of movement joints.

Figure 18.4 shows another case where a combination of monitoring was necessary to get the full picture. From visual inspection and distortion survey, it was not possible to be certain whether damage was the result of slope instability or vertical foundation subsidence due to a purely local and superficial cause. While damage increased, two inclinometers registered no horizontal movement, but levelling detected vertical foundation movement. It was safe to attend only to the more straightforward subsidence.

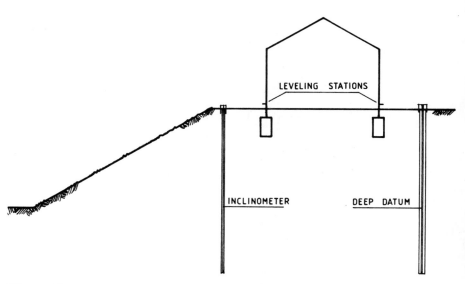

Figure 18.4 *Monitoring slope and building*

There are three possible remedies for active foundation movement: do nothing; or remove the cause and wait; or arrest the problem. These are obviously in ascending order of cost. Monitoring can offer economies if it accompanies the cheapest safe option. It will either prove the remedy chosen, or give early warning of continuing movement. Figure 18.5 shows a typical strap which would initially strengthen and stiffen the foundation. If monitoring detected a continuing movement, which needed arresting, the strap would be capable of supporting the building between future underpinning points. It goes without saying that the risks of minimal attention should be understood by everyone with an interest in the cost and outcome of the work.

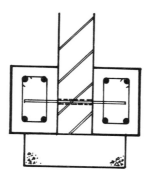

Figure 18.5 *Foundation strap*

In most cases which involve foundation movement, the period of monitoring should be at least 12 months. Once they have been installed, there may be sensible reasons for leaving the deep datum and stations in place as a guide to long-term maintenance. The most useful symptoms to monitor over a period of years are vertical foundation movement and (on older buildings) lean of external walls.

Although monitoring may direct and check remedial work, as an aid to diagnosis it should be considered as a last resort. If it is adopted as a regular tool, there is a temptation to assume that the investigation can afford to be less rigorous and interpretation more cautious, and the result is that the monitoring would spend time and money making up for previous inefficiency instead of improving the service. Nevertheless, the most rigorous of investigations can sometimes fail to reach confident conclusions. In such cases, or cases where there is a dispute between parties about cause, monitoring may be the best next step.

When monitoring is used for planned maintenance, the likely movements have to be anticipated, and interest centres on the load bearing walls whose behaviour can be defined by up, down and tilt, which are easy to measure.

Chapter 19

MANAGING LIABILITY

The limited aim of this chapter is to discuss ways of managing liability owed by an investigator to the client and third parties. Detailed aspects of liability: law; insurance; litigation; are not covered. If an investigation is not adequate there may be a cause for action in contract or in tort, or both.

The contract is the agreement, oral or written, to carry out an investigation for a fee. For a contract to be valid, the fee need not be defined at the time, although it is wise to do so. The investigator will, as part of any contract, be required to act with reasonable skill, and the two parties may define other obligations and limitations between themselves. Such obligations could become more important later, if refurbishment were to use information provided by the report, so the investigator should not give the impression that she or he has more than ordinary skill or is providing any sort of guarantee for the work. Normally the terms of a contract bind only the two parties, but if a collateral warranty is signed, the professional's duties will be extended to others.

Normally the contract period is six years, 12 years if signed under seal, but if there is provision for the contract to be assigned to others, future owners for example, its wording could have the effect of recommencing the contract period on re-assignment. For most investigations, the contract is simple and does not cause conflict. Tort offers greater scope for that. In tort, the investigator owes a duty of care to anyone relying on her or his judgement and may be sued if damage is suffered, provided the claimant can show that the damage has resulted from the investigator's negligence and there is a sufficient proximity of relationship between the two parties.

The Latent Damage Act 1986 set time limits within which a claim must be made. Every professional working in this field should have a basic knowledge of the Act because a proportion of instructions from clients will be, or will become, litigious and, until a solicitor is appointed, the investigator should safeguard others' interests. It would be wrong, for example, to let a prolonged investigation, perhaps involving many months of monitoring, time-bar possible recovery of costs for remedial works. Equally, advice given by an investigator is subject to the same time limits, and one irritating consequence is that records should be kept until the Act's long-stop has expired. Another is that only a fool practises without professional indemnity, and the cover should be continued after retirement, either by a continuation of the business or through a run-off policy.

A moment's carelessness, or alleged carelessness, may not lead to damage for some time, and the damage may not be immediately discoverable. When it is, it will take time to investigate and time to consider possible legal action. Ten years between act and action is not extreme. A decade is a very long time in law development, as the courts continually re-define the boundaries of negligence. Furthermore, only a minority of complaints are tried, the majority being resolved by insurance companies who temper their own prediction of the possible outcome at law with commercial considerations.

So today's act will be judged at an unknown time by unknown standards and with no certainty that either the technical or the legal principles will be properly tested. This offers no basis for prediction. One can only keep the client happy and try to avoid mistakes.

How hard one tries to avoid mistakes is a matter of personal conscience. The client pays for technical judgement and with any reasonably complex investigation one can form a succession of possible recommendations, each one launched a little further from the safe harbour of pure observation. There is no simple formula. Defensive practice is a fraud which appears in a number of disguises. Reports are sometimes produced which are mere lists of those building details which appear to have deviated from ideal practice, with no attempt to weigh their individual effect. Technical judgement is sometimes repressed altogether; alternatively, the advice may be given to correct every 'fault' observed, which is still a dereliction of judgement.

There is no harm in listing faults, but a list is no good on its own. Every building has at least a few faults, but only a minority cause damage. As an example, Figure 19.1 shows unreinforced concrete foundations which are too thin to be able, in theory, to spread the load to their full width. A report on masonry cracking listed this as the only foundation fault. The implication was that the failure to spread load was the cause of 12mm-wide cracking, presumably through abnormal settlement. A simple calculation would have proved that a restricted spread would still not have overloaded the soil, and simple observation should have dismissed the thought that the foundation was failing to cope with load transfer. A period of monitoring proved that clay heave was the problem. During this period the property became uninhabitable.

If a general rule can be made, bearing in mind there are so many different types of investigations and clients, then it might be to share one's deliberations

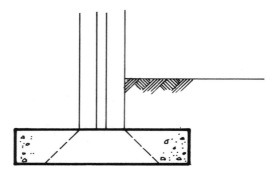

Figure 19.1   *Wide foundations*

about building faults with the client, not to jump from observation to recommendation, but to include the logic, the doubts and even the conflicts of evidence which eventually lead to opinion. This makes reporting more difficult, of course. There is often an uneasy feeling of compromise when putting technical thoughts into plain English. But the method of investigation itself, the gathering and testing of visual evidence, distortions and ground investigation in order to find a compatible theory for cause of damage, is easily understood by anyone, and a report which follows the stream of evidence should stand as a record of reasonable skill and care. So there is no reason why the method should not shape the report, at least for the more complex cases.

If the observations can only achieve hesitant interpretation, there is an opportunity to recommend further work (by specialists if necessary) or a period of monitoring. If the interpretation is clear but there are alternative courses of action, all the technically feasible ones should be discussed, followed by a reasoned recommendation. The client needs this information. There may be non-technical motives for adopting one of the courses discussed but not recommended.

A more formal way of recording reasonable skill and care is to adopt a quality scheme. It could be argued that this will invite higher expectations. The opinion of most professional idemnity insurers is that this possible drawback is outweighed by the fact that a well-devised and consistently executed quality scheme improves efficiency and reduces risk. The first requirement of a quality scheme is that it should suit the way the firm works; the firm should not try to adapt to anything rigid or alien. The first thing that a quality scheme does is to define quality. This is not easily done with any form of consultancy, let alone investigation.

Some firms set an implied quality by adopting an institute-approved checklist. Others may prepare their own. The latter has the advantage of being personally tailored and not ossified but improved by experience. The standard routine of visual inspection, distortion survey and ground investigation, with possible additions like desk study and drain test, could perhaps serve as a very broad checklist, without being too rigid.

Checklists are related to quality only indirectly. Ticking off items suggests that they were done but it provides no proof that they were done well. (If any such means of proof can be devised, litigation will become quicker, cheaper and rarer.) A performance specification for quality could be adopted, which would take the form of a statement such as: 'Our inspection will be sufficient to advise on the current safety of the structure. We will draw attention to any exceptional maintenance which is necessary to restore structural safety and structural serviceability. Where a query has been raised concerning an insured peril, we will give our opinion on the risk of damage arising from such a cause in the foreseeable future, although our opinion cannot be given in the form of a warranty.'

A quality scheme will insist on properly confirming the brief. That is the opportunity to anticipate the typical arguments which stem from misunderstandings about the scope, and even the type, of survey. A 'structural survey', for example, is usually done by a chartered surveyor and not a structural engineer, and the distinction is not obvious to every prospective house buyer. Limits imposed by restricted funds or the need to avoid inconvenience can, must, also be recorded. The client may like to be assured of the maximum cost and when the report will be ready.

A structural investigation, as distinct from the broader structural survey, will normally omit advice on non-structural matters such as condensation, and this should be made clear in the brief and again in the report. Some investigations may be limited to a particular location in the building or a specific structural problem, in which case the limitation has to be explained with extra care. If investigation is restricted to the roof space, for example, it would normally be simple enough to avoid inspection or comment on other areas, but not always, and the client cannot be expected to know this. For example, a roof which is badly tied may have caused spread; a visual inspection of at least the tops of supporting walls should be made. If, in a different case, roof stiffening is recommended, internal walls may be the ideal positions from which to strut additional purlins or binders, provided of course the walls are able to cope.

The main disadvantage of limited investigation can be illustrated by one last roof example: the unsupported chimney stack. So many chimneys have been unwisely altered or removed below the roof space. Should the investigators always check for support or make it clear that support has not been checked? If the roof is braced to the stack, which thereby takes on at least a secondary structural role, should that make checking obligatory?

Limited investigations are part of the service, but first the limitations must be realized by the investigator and then they must be carefully explained to the client. In fact they should be explained twice: first when the brief is accepted and again, if necessary, when the investigator realizes that the boundaries of inspection may have to be enlarged a little.

A quality scheme would ensure that the right person is assigned to carry out, or manage, the job. There should be a policy of defining the minimum professional qualifications and terms of experience for each type of investigation. This may seem pedantic to the firm doing the work, who would normally be well aware of everyone's capabilities, but it is reassuring to the client.

A procedure is then followed, and is recorded as having been followed. It should not be rigid enough to inhibit judgement. For routine surveys, the same checklist which was used to define quality (if it was) might form the outline of the procedure. Not every item on a checklist needs to be compulsory, but the use of the list gives the investigator the opportunity to note briefly why certain things were not able to be done, or were unnecessary in the circumstances. Instruments should be checked and calibrated at regular intervals.

It is good practice to have the report read by a colleague who is obliged to record her or his approval of it. This process should add less than five per cent to the cost. The checker, not having seen the building, will be at a disadvantage in any debate with the originator, so not every error will be spotted, but colleagues who are able to criticize each other constructively will certainly improve their own, and their firm's, consistency. If the occasional howler can be intercepted before it reaches the outside world, the system will pay for itself. It ceases to work if it degenerates into a rubber stamp routine.

Before closing the job, it should be confirmed that the original brief has been followed, allowing for whatever amendments were agreed along the way. The last requirement of a quality scheme is that a record should be kept confirming that the set plan or procedure, from instruction to closure, was substantially followed. This is a good discipline at the time and may possibly provide buried treasure for the future.

Regardless of any quality scheme, genuine arguments will continue to erupt over quality. No one is tolerant of professional uncertainty, except their own, and many people expect professional advice to be as exact as book-keeping. Most complaints arise from disappointed expectations.

The courts have the final word. They expect a professional person to apply no more than a reasonable degree of skill and state-of-the-art knowledge. This could hardly be fairer, although to the person being judged it can be suddenly terrifying when the original uncertainty is pierced by vivid hindsight. That is all the more reason to have a continuous policy towards liability, aimed at avoiding at least those complaints that can be avoided.

The reasonable degree of skill definition means that professionals are judged by peer standards. A chartered surveyor would be expected to recognize soil containing ash and brick fragments as fill. Fill can also consist of natural soil which has been dug up and redeposited, but unless such material were to look different from what could be expected in the vicinity, the chartered surveyor would not, in most circumstances, be expected to recognize it as fill. A chartered surveyor with exceptional skill or experience might do so, but not the average chartered surveyor. Obviously, a geotechnical engineer would not be forgiven for the same mistake.

It is wise to inform a client, who cannot be expected to know the boundaries of professional knowledge, when a boundary has been unexpectedly reached. It is essential not to stray beyond. These points are obvious on paper but camouflaged in real life. The investigator will not always know, at the time of confirming the brief, that part of the work will turn out to require specialist advice. That is unavoidable. The best that can be done is to warn the client as soon as it is known.

The specialist will normally take full responsibility for the specialist part of the investigation, but the instructing professional must be careful to:

- recommend an appropriate specialist
- give the specialist adequate instructions
- understand all the implications of the specialist's advice.

Even with these precautions the instructing professional is not entirely free of responsibility for the specialist advice. If the advice is poor, and the instructing professional should have realized that it was poor, then there may be a liability. The risk of that happening is greatest if the instructing professional passed on work which might be considered to be within his own province. For example, in most ordinary circumstances a chartered surveyor may safely discharge structural calculation to a chartered engineer and would remain innocent of the latter's mistakes, but the same might not be true if timber decay were delegated to a specialist whose recommendations turn out to be negligent, because chartered surveyors experienced in surveys are expected to have a reasonable amount of knowledge of the subject.

Many professionals have a standard disclaimer which they must quote in their report, as part of the professional indemnity policy conditions. Otherwise, disclaimers should be used sparingly. They may be judged unfair (Unfair Contract Terms Act, 1977), especially if they were not mentioned when the brief was confirmed, or were presented to a client who was unlikely to understand all their implications, or if they sought to exclude tasks and judgements which were not particularly difficult to carry out. Disclaimers may be more palatable if they are weaved into the narrative where they can be read in their proper context. For example, it is fair to say that a single trial hole will not necessarily reveal typical ground conditions, but a standard phrase to that effect has little impact, whereas a description of the trial-hole findings can include discussion on any particular site restrictions and a consideration of whether the ground in the vicinity is known to be variable, and so on. That would be honest and informative. (It also takes time. Not every technical report can afford such literary nicety.)

Returning to the limited investigation, but on a different facet: although it is only fair to record restrictions, one should still consider whether a disclaimer might later be considered unfair if a more widespread problem should have been evident to an experienced observer. On one occasion, for example, advice was sought from a civil engineer on the effect of vegetation on foundations. The terms of instruction were narrow and specific. Advice was based on a walkover. A complaint arose later, when the site was found to contain peaty soft alluvium, which was causing far more trouble than the vegetation. The low-lying position of the site, close to a bend in a river, gave some clue to the possible ground conditions, which might have been picked up at the time of the investigation, despite the specified restrictions. The complaint was resolved without testing its validity, but it is an example of what can happen even when the limitations are agreed in advance.

On the other hand, one has to avoid giving the impression of having done half a job. If certain areas or potential problems are excluded in the instructions, opinion should not be volunteered on the basis of a cursory inspection. That would be ill-considered gratuitous advice.

Gratuitous advice of any sort should be avoided. It increases liability without recompense, which might not please the professional indemnity insurers, and it tends to be made with a much shorter gestation than mainstream advice.

Advocacy (non-technical opinion) should be treated as gratuitous advice, unless the investigator has a legal qualification. Overt blame or crticisim should normally be avoided. Even terms like 'standard practice' should be tested for their truth before being used, in case the words unfairly imply someone's neglect.

One of the hardest balancing acts, when reporting, is to warn without alarming. Failure to warn may be considered negligent, even if the investigator has recognized a potential problem but has come to the honest opinion that the risk of it developing into a serious defect is very small. There is a temptation not to mention such risks at all, especially if the client is not used to reading technical reports, for fear of causing unnecessary anxiety. But unless the risk is negligible, which itself might not be an easy judgement, it seems better to discuss it openly and then give an opinion based on the balance of evidence.

The opposite of failure to warn is alarmist advice. Staying with the same slight risk example: if the professional decides to take no chances but to assume the worst will happen, and accordingly recommends costly preventive action, she or he could be held liable for its cost if it is later determined that the work was unnecessary.

The warn/alarm dilemma need not be fatal. If the evidence really is finely balanced, one ought to say so and recommend either further work or specialist advice or a period of monitoring. But in most cases a full discussion should give the client what she or he needs.

There is a hierarchy of client dissatisfaction, starting with nursed anxiety, and escalating through grumbling, questioning the advice given, withholding the fee, obtaining a second opinion and ending with litigation. The risk of conflict is reduced if the client's trust is gained early and maintained. This may mean taking more time to explain ideas and plans, and more frequent contact than is necessary to progress the work technically. For small jobs that is simply not always possible. With some clients it is not possible. The ideal is bound to lapse from time to time. But if a problem does arise later, the client who felt valued is inclined to turn first to the firm that carried out the work rather than a solicitor. There is an opportunity then to discuss the problem honestly and dispassionately, and to carry out further work, if necessary, to confirm or assuage any fears.

Many 'after sales' problems turn out to be trivial, but the effort put into solving them is still worthwhile compared with the time that would have been spent in conflict, not to mention the wear and tear on morale, and there is no reason why even a serious problem, for which liability has to be accepted, should not be handled without bitterness.

It goes without saying that professional indemnity insurers must be notified as soon as a possible liability is perceived. Acting without the insurer's approval, even with the best intentions, may prejudice their position, and force them to disclaim any liability they may have had. Failure to notify all claims, or circumstances which may give rise to claims, at the correct time (and, at the latest, prior to policy renewal) may invalidate the policy itself.

Lastly, if a problem is not resolved but the relationship has not broken down, it may be possible to agree on the appointment of a conciliator. Conciliation is quicker and cheaper than litigation or arbitration, but as it is not binding it only works when there is still something left of the original stock of goodwill.

Chapter 20

CONCLUSION

Steps to appraisal are outlined in Figure 20.1. Catastrophes demand urgent enquiry into the damaged condition of the building. This may conclude that the building is beyond rescue. If it can be rescued, a more leisurely assessment of distortions, reduced strength and lost integrity can be carried out as soon as safety is assured, and that will form the appraisal which is then the basis for remedial work. Safe buildings can afford to start with the leisurely assessment.

All causes of damage have their characteristic life cycles. Identifying the cause is only a short step away from recommending action. The cause of damage may be extinct, short lived, progressive or recurrent. An extinct cause may have left a legacy of reduced strength or robustness which may need restoring, but beyond that, any attention is cosmetic.

If the cause remains active, the first question is: can it be allowed to run its course? One of the most troublesome examples of that question is heave damage following tree removal. The heave can be relied upon to work its way out eventually, but whether it will do so quietly or dramatically is often difficult to predict or even monitor. Subsidence, on the other hand, is always progressive until the cause is removed.

That leads to the next question: can the building cope unaided with the transition from active cause to stable conditions? In the case of subsidence caused by, for example, leaking drains, further movement is likely while the loosened ground packs down to a stable density, and the answer to the question therefore depends on how loose the soil is and how stiff and strong the structure is.

Clay/tree subsidence is likely to be followed, when the cause is removed, by a reversal of movement, in other words recovery. The answer to whether the building will cope then depends on how much recovery is expected. The same

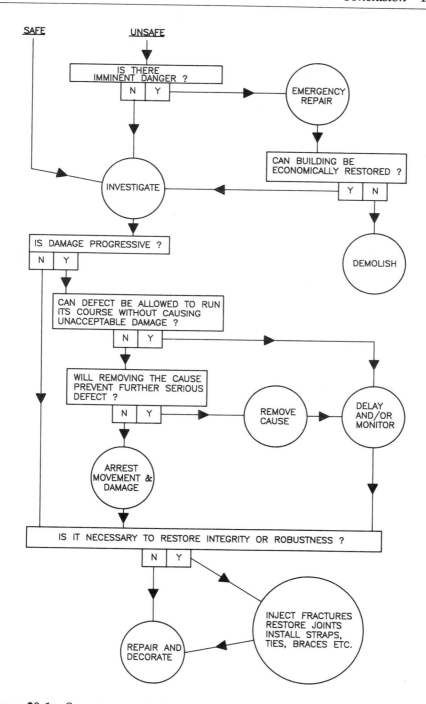

Figure 20.1   *Steps to appraisal*

question can be applied to an undamaged building facing a risk which has just been established. Unstable ground, for example, may be likely to cause damage; the removal of its potential would avoid any damage at all. To the extent that technical argument can influence it, action would be determined by comparing the perceived risk and its consequences with the cost of its elimination.

The stage between removal of cause and arrival of stability can be informed by monitoring, and the damage during that stage can in appropriate circumstances be controlled by judicious strengthening and stiffening if that is judged to be both an economic alternative and preferable to arresting the problem altogether.

Whether the consequence is avoided or tolerated, the final steps are to restore lost integrity and robustness, only if necessary, and then to carry out the normal repairs and redecorations. At that stage, there will be supplementary questions if the building is to be altered in its form or use, in which case the restoration would probably include some improvement.

The vital steps are the initial ones. Technical decisions flow from the causes of damage, and their accurate assessment is the cornerstone of structural appraisal.

Appraisal is frustrated by the difficulties of obtaining adequate evidence; it is promoted by methodical cross-checking. The reward of accurate appraisal is economy. Problems are found sooner, because even slight damage can be diagnosed if the evidence cross-checks; and unnecessary work is avoided, because innocent faults and extinct damage can be left alone.

Repeated over a number of investigations, economy in structural appraisal provides a quiet service to our stock of traditional buildings by keeping them alive without raiding funds better spent on their appearance and comfort.

Glossary

Angular distortion Rotational strain caused by differential movement. In masonry, it is characteristically accompanied by tapered cracking and can be measured by distortion survey (see diagram below).

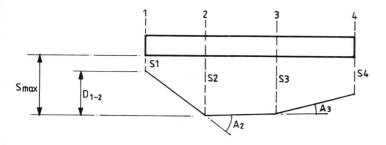

S1, S2, S3, S4	:	TOTAL SETTLEMENT OR SUBSIDENCE AT THESE POINTS
S max	:	MAXIMUM SETTLEMENT OR SUBSIDENCE
D 1-2	:	DIFFERENTIAL SETTLEMENT OR SUBSIDENCE BETWEEN POINTS 1 2
A 2	:	ANGULAR DISTORTION AT 2
A 3	:	ANGULAR DISTORTION AT 3

Ashlar High quality stonework, with regular though not necessarily uniform coursing, and usually fine jointing.

Boroscope Instrument for illumination and remote inspection, typically used for examining wall cavities.

Clay lump Type of earth wall (see pp. 150–1).

Cob Type of earth wall (see pp. 150–1).

Consolidation The reduction in soil volume caused by expulsion of pore water and/or compression of the soil skeleton under pressure. The pressure may be from applied loading, such as a building, or self-weight, or both.

Contraction Shortening caused by drying shrinkage or reduction in moisture content or fall in temperature.

Creep Strain which is still increasing, but at a decreasing rate: in other words each successive period sees less movement than the previous. It is a characteristic of many distortions which affect buildings, including settlement on fill or organic soil, the spread of untied roofs and the deflection of timber beams.

Differential settlement Difference in settlement between two points on a wall or foundation (see diagram on p. 199).

Differential subsidence Difference in subsidence between two points on a wall or foundation (see diagram on p.199).

Expansion Lengthening caused by an increase in moisture content or rise in temperature or (in the case of clay brickwork) early irreversible moisture movement.

Flexural strength Resistance to damage caused by bending.

Heartwood Older, usually darker, wood from the interior of the tree. It is stronger and more durable than sapwood (q.v.), and more resistant to infestation.

Jetty The projection of the floor of a mediaeval timber frame building beyond the storey below.

Kentledge Dead weight used for load testing.

Lateral heave Heave pressure which acts in the horizontal direction.

Leaching The removal of the small particles of soil from the soil matrix by the action of travelling water. Silt and fine sand are the most vulnerable particles.

Peak particle velocity The maximum speed of a vibrating particle during its cycle of movement.

Piezometer A tube inserted and sealed into the ground to monitor the ground-water level or pore pressure at a specific position and depth.

Plasticity A measure of the soil's response to moisture content, which is an indicator of soil properties (see pp. 53–56).

Pisé Type of earth wall (see pp. 150–1).

Restraint The prevention or reduction of movement imposed on one element by another. Walls which would otherwise be slender benefit from restraint by other walls, floors and roofs. By preventing free movement due to shrinkage or expansion, restraint may impose stress and cause damage.

Sapwood Younger, usually lighter, wood from the outside of the tree. It is weaker and less durable than heartwood, and less resistant to infestation.

Sedimentation test A laboratory test for establishing the clay content of a soil. Larger particles can be separated by sieve analysis.

Settlement Downward movement caused by consolidation of the soil under load. The load would normally be applied by the building, but it could arise from another source such as fill placed to raise the ground level (see diagram on p. 199).

Snap header A brick which appears as a header but which has been halved in length so that it lies entirely within one skin.

Sole plate Horizontal timber which forms the bottom member of a timber frame. With mediaeval timber frame, it is laid directly on the soil, below ground level, or else on a stone plinth. With modern timber frame, it is the horizontal timber to which each panel is fixed at floor level.

Stylobate Stone pad set into the ground and supporting mediaeval timber post.

Subsidence The downward movement caused by consolidation of the soil under the influence of factors other than applied load. Two frequent examples are clay shrinkage caused by reduction in moisture content and collapse of coarse soil caused by leaching (see diagram on p. 199).

Venting Reduction of explosive pressure caused by removal of a window, door or partition.

Wytchert Type of earth wall (see pp. 150–1).

Further Reading

Addleson, L., *Building Failures: A Guide to Diagnosis, Remedy and Prevention*, 2nd ed., Butterworth Architecture, London 1989, 167pp.

Ashurst, J. & N., *Practical Building Conservation,* Vols 1 to 5, Gower Technical Press, Aldershot, 1989.

Bell, F.G., *Engineering Properties of Soils and Rocks*, Butterworths, London 1981, 149pp.

Bravery, A.F. and Carey, J.K., *Recognising Wood Rot and Insect Damage in Buildings*, BRE Report, HMSO, London 1987, 120pp.

Bromhead, E.N., *The Stability of Slopes*, Surrey University Press, London 1986, 373pp.

Brown, R.J., *The English Country Cottage*, Robert Hale, London 1979, 272pp.

Brunskill, R.W., *Illustrated Handbook of Vernacular Architecture*, 3rd ed., Faber & Faber, London 1987, 256pp.

Brunskill, R.W., *Timber Building in Britain*, Gollancz, London 1985, 240pp.

Building Research Establishment (BRE) Digest 251, *Assessment of Damage in Low-Rise Buildings with Particular Reference to Progressive Foundation Movement*, HMSO, London, July 1981, 8pp.

BRE Digests and Defect Action Sheets, current full set, HMSO, London.

CIRIA Report 111, *Structural Renovation of Traditional Buildings*, CIRIA, London 1986, 98pp.

Cornes, D.L., *Design Liability in the Construction Industry*, 3rd ed., BSP Professional Books, Oxford 1989, 295pp.

Cunnington, P., *Care for Old Houses*, Prism Alpha, Sherbourne 1984, 255pp.

Cutler, D.F. and Richardson, I.B.K., *Tree Roots and Buildings*, 2nd ed., Longman Scientific & Technical, Harlow 1989, 71pp.

Directory of Mines and Quarries, British Geological Survey, Keyworth, Nottingham 1988.

Harris, R., *Discovering Timber-Framed Buildings,* 2nd ed., Shire Publications Ltd., Aylesbury, Buckinghamshire 1979, 96pp.

Highfield, D., *Rehabilitation and Re-use of Old Buildings,* Spon, London 1987, 186pp.

Institution of Civil Engineers, *Ground Subsidence*, Thomas Telford, London 1977, 99pp.

Little, A.J., *Foundations*, Edward Arnold Ltd, London 1961, 364pp.

NHBC, *The Handbook for Registered House-Builders, Technical Requirements for the Design and Construction of Dwellings*, revised November 1988, London.

Peters, J.E.C., *Discovering Traditional Farm Buildings*, Shire Publications Ltd, Aylesbury, Buckinghamshire 1981, 80pp.

Robson, P., 'Deep datum monitoring as a guide to economic repair', *Construction Repair*, Palladian Press, Windsor, August 1987, **1**, (3), 8–11.

Structural Survey, Henry Stewart Publications, London, quarterly.

Tomlinson, M.J. *Foundation Design and Construction*, 5th ed., Longman Scientific & Technical, Harlow 1986, 793pp.

Index